HISTORY & GEOGRAPHY 804

A Firm Foundation (1789–1820)

LIFEPAC Test is located in the center of the booklet. Please remove before starting the unit.

Author:

Theresa Buskey, B.A., J.D.

Editor:

Alan Christopherson, M.S.

Westover Studios Design Team:

Phillip Pettet, Creative Lead

Teresa Davis, DTP Lead

Nick Castro

Andi Graham

Jerry Wingo

Alpha Omega

PUBLICATIONS

804 N. 2nd Ave. E.
Rock Rapids, IA 51246-1759

A Firm Foundation (1789–1820)

Introduction

The first forty years after the ratification of the Constitution was a time of foundation building. The new Constitution had to be transformed from ideas on paper to a practical, working government. Even with a good plan, a weak original government would set precedents that would be hard to change. It was up to first president, George Washington, and his advisors to use the blueprint of the Constitution to build a good foundation for the structure of the United States.

The early years of our nation were complicated by events in Europe. The French Revolution began in 1789. The king of France was overthrown and executed. The Revolution degenerated into a blood-bath called the Reign of Terror (1793-94). A war began in Europe as other monarchs tried to interfere. Finally, General Napoleon Bonaparte seized power in France (1799) and conquered much of Europe. He was defeated by an alliance led by Britain (1813) and went into exile (1814). In 1815 he returned to be defeated again.

The war put America in a difficult position. France had been America's ally in the Revolution, but Britain was America's biggest trading partner. Both sides had interfered with American trade during the long years of conflict, but the actions of the British were especially infuriating. The hard-pressed American leaders did not want to get into a European war. By 1812, the long-suffering Americans could take no more; war was declared on Britain. The second war of independence, the War of 1812, finished laying the foundation of America. With the foundation laid, the country built toward its future.

Objectives

Read these objectives. The objectives tell you what you will be able to do when you have successfully completed this LIFEPAC. When you have finished this LIFEPAC, you should be able to:

1. Describe the important events of the first five presidential administrations.

2. Describe the Great Seal of the United States.

3. Describe the course and nature of America's problems with Britain that led to the War of 1812.

4. Describe the growth, policies, and decline of the Federalist Party.

5. Describe the growth and policies of the Democratic-Republican Party.

6. Describe the course and results of the War of 1812.

7. Describe how America changed after the War of 1812.

8. Describe the development of the power of the Supreme Court under John Marshall.

9. Explain the reasons behind U.S. policy decisions from 1789 to the early 1820s.

Survey the LIFEPAC. Ask yourself some questions about this study and write your questions here.

_____
_____
_____
_____
_____
_____
_____
_____
_____
_____
_____
_____
_____
_____
_____
_____
_____

1. FEDERALIST ERA

The Federalists led the victorious battle for the Constitution after the Constitutional Convention. When the first government was formed under the new plan in 1789, it was dominated by the same Federalists. They controlled the U.S. government through the Washington and Adams administrations, but they were driven from power in 1801 when Thomas Jefferson became president under the Democratic-Republican Party.

The republic faced many difficulties in the first twelve years under the Constitution. Washington had to establish exactly what all the descriptions of his duties meant and what the newly created post required of him. Alexander Hamilton, the first secretary of the treasury, had to repair the poor state of the nation's finances. A rebellion broke out against the new taxes which such repairs required. America had to deal with the French Revolution and a European war. Trade problems threatened war with both Britain and France. Controversy brewed over a treaty with Britain and a bribery scandal with France. Finally, the Federalists began their own decline by threatening freedom of speech in an attempt to control the passions of the era.

SECTION OBJECTIVES

Review these objectives. When you have completed this section, you should be able to:

1. Describe the important events of the first five presidential administrations.

2. Describe the Great Seal of the United States.

3. Describe the course and nature of America's problems with Britain that led to the War of 1812.

4. Describe the growth, policies, and decline of the Federalist Party.

5. Describe the growth and policies of the Democratic-Republican Party.

9. Explain the reasons behind U.S. policy decisions from 1789 to the early 1820s.

VOCABULARY

Study these words to enhance your learning success in this section.

agrarian (u grar′ ē an). Concerning agriculture or rural matters.

bond (bond). A certificate issued by a government or company which promises to pay back, with interest; the money borrowed from the buyer of the certificate.

nominal (nom′ i nal). In name only; not real or actual.

nullify (nul′ i fī). To deprive of legal force; make void.

partisan (pär′ ti zan). A very strong supporter of a party, cause, or faction.

repudiation (ri pyoo′ dē ā′ shun). The act of rejecting the validity of something.

Note: *All vocabulary words in this LIFEPAC appear in* **boldface** *print the first time they are used. If you are not sure of the meaning when you are reading, study the definitions given.*

Pronunciation Key: h**a**t, **ā**ge, c**ã**re, f**ä**r; l**e**t, **ē**qual, t**ė**rm; **i**t, **ī**ce; h**o**t, **ō**pen, **ô**rder; **oi**l; **ou**t; c**u**p, p**u̇**t, r**ü**le; **ch**ild; lo**ng**; **th**in; /ŦH/ for **th**en; /zh/ for mea**s**ure; /u/ or /ə/ represents /a/ in **a**bout, /e/ in tak**e**n, /i/ in penc**i**l, /o/ in lem**o**n, and /u/ in circ**u**s.

AMERICA from **1789** to **1820**

George Washington
1789–1797

John Adams
1797–1801
Federalist

Thomas Jefferson
1801–1809
Democratic-Republican

James Madison
1809–1817
Democratic-Republican

James Monroe
1817–1825
Democratic-Republican

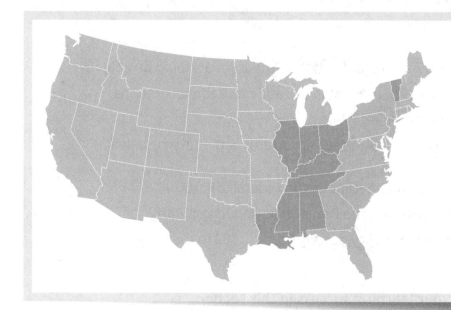

STATES ADMITTED TO THE UNION

Vermont	1791
Kentucky	1792
Tennessee	1796
Ohio	1803
Louisiana	1812
Indiana	1816
Mississippi	1817
Alabama	1819
Illinois	1819

POPULATION of the United States of America

1820 | 9,638,453

1790 | 3,929,000

Washington's First Term

There was never any doubt as to who would be elected as the first president of the United States. George Washington was the one person who had the public trust and the stature to take the job. He had the support of both the Federalists and Anti-Federalists. It can reasonably be argued that the position was created with him in mind. The Constitution required each state to choose electors who would then choose a president. When the vote was counted in April of 1789, the tally was unanimous for Washington. (He was the only president to receive a unanimous electoral vote). John Adams was chosen as vice president.

The same qualities that made Washington a great general also made him a superb first president. He did not like politics and accepted the presidency only because he felt the nation needed him. He commanded the respect of his subordinates and gave his tremendous prestige to the new post. He was careful, fair, and methodical. He chose wise counselors and listened to them before making his decisions. He provided the stability and thoughtful leadership the new nation so desperately needed in those early years.

Inauguration. Washington received word of his election at his home in Mount Vernon, Virginia. He immediately left on the long journey to New York City, which was America's temporary capital. He was greeted all along the route by cheering crowds. He took the oath of office on the balcony of Federal Hall, overlooking Wall Street, on April 30, 1789. He then gave an inaugural address in the chambers of the Senate.

Washington set a formal tone for the new office, mainly because of his own rather formal personality. He would bow, not shake hands, to greet visitors. He dressed richly and drove about in a handsome coach. Visitors could see him during his weekly open house or make an appointment. His wife Martha held a formal reception every Friday evening that the president attended. The office of president was less than a king, but more than a simple politician.

| George Washington's inauguration

Cabinet. The new Congress created three departments to help the president run the government: foreign affairs (state), war, and treasury. An attorney general, the attorney for the government, was added later. Washington choose men he knew and trusted to head these departments. They came to be his personal advisors and eventually met together to discuss decisions, forming the president's cabinet.

Washington stayed out of **partisan** politics as much as he could, but he recognized the conflicts of the day and represented both sides in his cabinet. Thomas Jefferson was the first secretary of state. He was a firm believer in a weak federal government, an **agrarian** country, and rule by the "common people." He eventually became the leader of the Democratic-Republican Party. Alexander Hamilton was the first secretary of the treasury. He was a Federalist leader who believed in a strong central government, a commercial nation, and rule by the "elite." The other cabinet members were Secretary of War Henry Knox and Attorney General Edmund Randolph.

Washington did not officially attach himself to either of the new political parties. However, mainly on the basis of Hamilton's arguments, he supported much of the Federalist agenda. As a result, Washington came under attack from the Anti-Federalists, who eventually developed into the Democratic-Republican Party.

Finances. The main problem facing the new government was the same one they had faced under the Articles of Confederation—money. The nation was deeply in debt and had no stable currency. Hamilton proposed the government pay the debt at full value and assume the Revolutionary War debts of the states as well. Hamilton intended to build the power of the federal government by establishing it financially and having the people look to it, not the state governments, for their money.

There was a tremendous amount of opposition to Hamilton's plan. Few people believed the **bonds** issued by the Revolutionary government would ever be paid. The war veterans and people who originally held the bonds had sold them for a fraction of what they were worth. Most were owned by wealthy men who could afford to hold them and wait. Many felt that it was unfair to give the profit to these men. Hamilton wanted the support of these wealthy citizens for the new government. He wanted to give the rich and well-born a stake in the new system.

Most of the southern states had already paid off their war debts. They objected to also paying off the northern debts through the federal government. Eventually, they agreed to the plan in exchange for placing the new national capital in the south, on the Potomac River between Maryland and Virginia. The rest of Hamilton's plan was accepted because Congress believed that a government should pay its lawful debts and knew it would be impossible to find the original owners of the bonds.

The third part of Hamilton's plan called for the establishment of a national bank. The bank would be partially owned by the government and would be used to deposit government funds. It also would issue a stable paper currency backed by the deposits in the bank.

The bank ran into violent opposition in Congress. Most of the supporters came from the north which favored a strong currency and bank to build trade and manufacturing. State's rights advocates did not want a large central bank which would compete with their state banks. The measure was passed after a heated debate and was sent to Washington for his signature.

Washington was deeply concerned about whether the bill was constitutional. He asked Jefferson (against) and Hamilton (for) to each give him a written opinion on the matter. Jefferson argued that the Constitution did not specifically authorize a bank. He favored a "strict construction" of the Constitution. The government could only do things specifically allowed by the Constitution, a position that would have severely limited federal power. Hamilton, on the other hand, persuasively argued for a "loose construction." The Constitution said that the Congress could pass any laws "necessary and proper" to carrying out the powers of the government. Since the government was authorized to collect taxes, a bank was both necessary and proper to fulfill that function. Washington agreed with Hamilton and signed the bill.

Money to pay the debts and finance the bank came from taxes. The primary tax of that day was the tariff, a tax on goods imported from other countries. A tariff also made foreign goods more expensive, thus protecting the few American manufacturers. This fit well with Hamilton's far-sighted plan for America to become a manufacturing nation. Congress also passed an excise tax on distilled liquor to supplement the tariff income.

The prosperity of the new government depended on trade which produced tariff income. Most of America's trade was with Britain. Thus, Hamilton and the Federalists came to favor England over France in foreign policy. This created yet another difference with Jefferson's supporters who favored France, a country that found itself in the middle of its own revolution.

Match these people.

1.1	_____ George Washington	a.	secretary of war
1.2	_____ John Adams	b.	attorney general
1.3	_____ Thomas Jefferson	c.	chosen unanimously by the electors
1.4	_____ Alexander Hamilton	d.	vice president
1.5	_____ Edmund Randolph	e.	secretary of state
1.6	_____ Henry Knox	f.	secretary of the treasury

Answer these questions.

1.7 What were Hamilton's three main proposals for the nation's finances?

a. _____

b. _____

c. _____

1.8 What did the southern states get in exchange for the federal government taking over the state's debts?

_____

1.9 What form of taxation was the main source of income for the new government?

_____

1.10 Why did some people not want the war bonds to be paid at full value?

_____

_____

_____

Put an *H* beside the policies supported by Hamilton and a *J* beside those supported by Jefferson.

1.11 _____ favored Britain

1.12 _____ strong central government

1.13 _____ agrarian society

1.14 _____ favored France

1.15 _____ weak federal government

1.16 _____ "strict construction" of Constitution

1.17 _____ "loose construction" of Constitution

1.18 _____ commercial society

THE GREAT SEAL

Nations are represented by symbols. The most famous symbol of the United States is our flag, the Stars and Stripes. Another important symbol is the Great Seal, which was adopted in 1782 by the nation's first government, the Second Continental Congress. Most people have probably seen the front or "obverse" of the Great Seal of the United States. It appears on federal buildings, vehicles, laws, and documents as well as coins and currency. The back or "reverse" is less well known, but it does appear on the back of the one-dollar bill. The Seal is rich with symbolism, much of which refers to the Christian foundation of our nation.

| The Great Seal of the United States

The Obverse of the Great Seal

On the obverse side of the seal are these symbols:

1. The Crest: At the top of the seal is a cluster of thirteen white stars on a blue field, which represents the original thirteen states. A ring of golden light is breaking through a white cloud which surrounds the stars. This light is a symbol of God's constant protection and guidance.

2. The National Coat of Arms: The remainder of the seal is our nation's coat of arms, which consists of these symbols;

   a. American Eagle: The eagle was selected to represent the United States because of its dignity, size, strength, and majestic appearance. The head and tail feathers are white, the claws and beak are yellow. Franklin wanted our symbol to be a turkey, but he was wisely outvoted by the committee.

   b. Shield: On the eagle's breast is a shield. The solid blue bar at the top represents the national government (originally just Congress). The seven white stripes and six red stripes stand for the first thirteen states.

   c. Scroll and Motto: Held by the eagle's beak is a golden scroll on which are written these words in Latin:
   E PLURIBUS UNUM
   The English translation of this motto is "One out of many." Many states make up the one nation, the United States of America.

   d. Thirteen Arrows: The eagle's left talon is clutching a bundle of thirteen arrows. This suggests that we will defend our nation.

   e. Olive Branch: The eagle's right talon is clutching a green olive branch with thirteen blue-tinted olives. The olive branch is a symbol of peace. Since the right side is considered to be more important, holding the olive branch in the right talon indicates that the United States prefers peace to war. The eagle is also facing the peace side rather than the war side.

The Reverse of the Great Seal

This part of the Great Seal is not as well known. The parts and their meanings are:

1. The Pyramid: In the center of the Seal is a pyramid built on the earth with a blue sky background. On the base of the pyramid are the Roman numerals MDCCLXXVI (1776), the year our nation was born. Thirteen layers of stone are in the pyramid, representing the original thirteen states. The pyramid is unfinished, indicating that our nation will continue to grow. The pyramid shape symbolizes the strength and stability of the United States.

2. The Eye: Above the pyramid is a large eye within a blue triangle surrounded by a golden light. The eye is a symbol that God is watching over our nation. The light represents God's glory and majesty.

3. Latin Mottoes:

   a. *ANNUIT COEPTIS* is written across the top of the Seal in golden letters. This means: *He (God) has favored our undertaking.*

   b. *NOVUS ORDO SECLORUM* is written in black letters on a golden scroll across the bottom. This means: *A new order of the ages.*

The Great Seal

On the Great Seal.

1.19 Name five ways that the original thirteen states are represented.

a. _____   b. _____

c. _____   d. _____

e. _____

1.20 Name two ways the presence of God is represented.

a. _____

b. _____

1.21 Why is the olive branch in the eagle's right talon? _____

_____

1.22 What does "E Pluribus Unum" mean? _____

Washington's Second Term

Washington wanted to retire after his first term. However, his friends urged him to stay on for another term for the sake of the country. He agreed and was unanimously re-elected in 1792. In March 1793, he was inaugurated in Philadelphia, which was the new temporary capital. Adams also returned as vice president.

European War. Washington received word of a general war in Europe a month into his second term. France was at war with Britain, Austria, Spain, and Prussia. France had been America's primary ally during the Revolution, and the treaty of alliance obligated the U.S. to aid them now. However, that treaty had been signed with the king of France who had been executed in the French Revolution. Supporters of the French Revolution wanted to honor the treaty. But even Jefferson was reluctant to get into another war. The Federalists feared the effect that war with Britain would have on trade and urged neutrality.

America was not strong militarily or politically. There was no army, and the new government had only been in place for four years. The pressures of a war could easily destroy all that had been built. Washington decided that the nation could not afford to be involved in a European war and issued a Proclamation of Neutrality on April 22nd. This continued to be the policy of the U.S. for most of the remaining years of this long war. American leaders desperately tried to keep out of the conflict as long as they could in order to buy time for their nation to grow strong.

Citizen Genêt. The republican government of France sent a new representative to America in April of 1793. He was Citizen (the title used by all in the Revolution) Edmond Genêt, an enthusiastic and tactless man. He had been commissioned to renew the treaty of friendship with America and obtain a new trade treaty. What he did was create a huge mess for Washington.

Genêt was received with joy by French supporters in America. He began at once to commission privateers to attack British shipping from American ports. He also tried to organize expeditions against the Spanish and British lands in America. Washington received him coolly, but Genêt did not take the hint. He ignored the Neutrality Proclamation and appealed to the American people to support France in the war. All this activity threatened to convince Britain that America was not truly neutral. Washington finally asked France to recall Genêt. He was stripped of his authority by a new government in France and stayed in the U.S. for fear of execution upon his return. American neutrality held.

Whiskey Rebellion. The excise tax passed by Congress during Washington's first administration had hit the northwestern farmers hard. It was difficult for these frontier farmers to make a profit shipping their grain to markets in the east because of the cost. Therefore, they routinely distilled their grain into liquor which was easier to transport and provided a good profit. The excise tax was immensely unpopular among these men and sparked a frontier revolt called the Whiskey Rebellion.

The Whiskey Rebellion began in 1794 in western Pennsylvania. The farmers there drew up resolutions against the tax, attacked the tax collectors, and terrorized court officials. The governor refused to act, so Washington called out the militia in the other states to enforce the law. The response was an army of over 13,000 men, more than Washington had for much of the Revolution. The rebellion scattered, and Washington pardoned the two culprits who were caught. The government's firmness made rebellious individuals use voting, rather than fighting, as the best means for pursuing their goals.

Problem with Britain. During his second term, Washington had to deal with the increasing problems with Great Britain. England still kept possession of several western forts in U.S. territory. It continued to support the Native American population there, hoping to use them as a buffer between the U.S. and Canada. As the war progressed with France, Britain began

| John Jay, negotiator with the British

seizing U.S. ships and cargoes trading with France or French colonies. The British also would search U.S. ships for British sailors who had become U.S. citizens. These men and many others who had never been British citizens were "impressed" or forced into serving in the British navy. Americans were outraged by this treatment of their vessels and citizens.

Jay's Treaty. Washington, hoping to avoid a war, and at the urging of the Federalists, sent John Jay to London to negotiate a settlement. He succeeded in obtaining a treaty in late 1794. The British agreed to evacuate the American forts, pay some compensation for the seized cargoes, and improve U.S. trading rights with Britain. However, the agreement mentioned nothing about ending their interference with American shipping or impressing of American sailors. The treaty restated the obligation of Americans to pay back debts owed to Britain from before the Revolution. Washington, believing it was the best he could get, submitted it to the Senate for approval.

The treaty was violently unpopular. Westerners were angry that it did not deal with the English support of the Native Americans. Southerners were angry that it did not require Britain to pay for slaves taken during the Revolution. Supporters of France saw it as a rejection of the nation's obligation to the French people. Patriotic Americans were angered by the extension of trade with a nation that freely mistreated American citizens. Even Hamilton, who needed the treaty to prevent a war and keep his financial system on track, did not like it. However, the pro-British, pro-trade Federalists dominated the Senate and after weeks of debate, it was approved. The nation was able to avoid a war for the time being.

Jay's Treaty did have one positive effect. Spain became nervous over the possibility of a British-American alliance in North America and settled some of her outstanding disputes with the U.S. A Spanish-American treaty was signed in 1795. It gave Americans the right to use the Mississippi and bring their goods through the Spanish-controlled port of New Orleans without paying any duty. It set the southern boundary of the U.S. and contained a Spanish promise to control Native Americans in their territory. This treaty helped restore the damaged national pride.

Farewell Address. Washington had come under savage attack for his policies and Jay's Treaty during his second administration. He was weary of public life and discouraged by the division of the government into factions. Washington believed political parties were a threat to the unity of the nation, but he had been unable to prevent them. Jefferson had even resigned from the cabinet because of Washington's support of Hamilton.

Washington announced that he would not accept re-election again. He set a "two-terms only" precedent which was followed by every president until Franklin Roosevelt in 1940. (After that, the president was limited to two terms by a constitutional amendment). He also published the *Farewell Address* that issued two warnings to the American people. The first was to avoid party politics. This was ignored. The second was that America should avoid all permanent alliances like the one made with France during the Revolution since they would draw us into foreign wars. This admonition became a key part of American foreign policy for generations. America did not sign a permanent military alliance again until after World War II (1938-1945).

 Complete the following.

1.23 Washington reacted to the War in Europe in 1793 by issuing the _____

_____ .

1.24 In 1793 France was at war with _____

_____ .

1.25 The French republican representative to the U.S. in 1793 was (including his title)

_____ .

1.26 Name three things the French envoy did that threatened U.S. neutrality.

a. _____

b. _____

c. _____

1.27 What were the problems America was having with Britain?

a. _____

b. _____

c. _____

d. _____

1.28 What did the British agree to do under Jay's Treaty?

a. _____

b. _____

c. _____

1.29 Why did so many Americans object to Jay's Treaty?

_____

_____

_____

1.30 What was the Whiskey Rebellion and how was it settled?

_____

_____

_____

1.31 What two things did Washington recommend that Americans avoid in the *Farewell Address*?

_____ and _____

1.32 Washington set the precedent that the president serves _____ terms.

Adams Administration

Election of 1796. The elections of George Washington had been uncontested. In the election of 1796, however, there were three candidates. Hamilton was too unpopular to run as a candidate, so the Federalist faction supported John Adams or Thomas Pinckney (backed by Hamilton). The Democratic-Republicans supported Thomas Jefferson. With Washington no longer acting as a unifying factor, the verbal mud flew back and forth, further separating the two developing political parties. Adams won by three electoral votes. The system at the time did not take political parties into account, and the runner-up in electoral votes, Thomas Jefferson, received the vice presidency. The messy situation of having a president from one political party and his vice president from another was eventually prevented by the 12th Amendment to the Constitution, adopted in 1804.

John Adams was a lawyer from Massachusetts and had been an active participant in the political end of the Revolution. He had worked to oppose the Stamp Act, followed his conscience in defending the British soldiers responsible for the Boston Massacre, served in the First and Second Continental Congress, and represented America in Europe during the Revolutionary War. He assisted in the negotiations with Britain at the end of the war and was America's first ambassador to the former mother country. He returned home in 1788 and was selected to serve under Washington as vice president.

Adams was a very capable statesman but tended to be cold and sharp in person. He and Thomas Jefferson had become friends during the Revolution. Their political differences would temporarily end their relationship until after both had retired from office. Adams and Hamilton did not get along at all. Adams represented the moderate part of the Federalist party while Hamilton's views were more extreme. This split would do tremendous damage to the Federalist Party.

Adams kept all of Washington's cabinet when he took office in 1797. Hamilton had resigned earlier, but most of the other cabinet members kept him informed of their activities and relied on his advice. This further aggravated the problems between the two men and their supporters. Adams also inherited from Washington the problems in Europe, and those would dominate his time in office.

XYZ Affair. The Jay Treaty had triggered a crisis with France. The French saw it as a **repudiation** of the French-American treaty signed during the Revolution. The latest French government, the Directory, began to seriously harass U.S. trade and insultingly refused to receive a new American ambassador. Adams sent a special three-man delegation to France to try to resolve the dispute.

The American delegation arrived in France in 1797 and was approached by three representatives of Talleyrand, the French foreign minister. These three coolly requested a huge bribe for both the Directory and Talleyrand before negotiations could even begin! The Americans firmly refused and left. They filed a full report with Adams, calling the three French representatives X, Y, and Z.

The XYZ Affair triggered a tremendous outcry when it became public in America. The insult to the national honor excited everyone. The extreme Federalists under Hamilton led the call for war. Taxes were raised to improve the navy and army. An aging George Washington was named as the **nominal** head of the army, with Alexander Hamilton in actual command. Americans put aside their own differences, and even Democratic-Republicans joined in the cry of "Millions for defense but not one cent for tribute."

Through it all, Adams kept his head. He realized the new nation could not afford a war. He proceeded with preparations, but with the support of the moderate Federalists, never called for declaration of war. An undeclared war went on between the ships of both sides for about two years. Finally, Talleyrand realized he could not afford to add America to the list of countries fighting France. He let Adams know that a new delegation would be received properly.

Convention of 1800. Adams authorized a new delegation to go to France in 1799 over the severe objections of much of his own party. The government in France had changed yet again by the time the Americans arrived. Napoleon Bonaparte was now the dictator of France, and he wanted to clear up foreign disputes to leave himself a free hand in Europe. The two sides negotiated (without bribes) the Convention of 1800. The Convention officially ended the old French-American treaty of alliance and temporarily settled the differences between the two nations. Adams had won the peace, but his refusal to give in to war hysteria cost him his popularity. He deserves a great deal of credit for stubbornly putting his country ahead of his political ambitions.

Alien and Sedition Acts. The Federalists had regained strength in Congress after the XYZ Affair. They took advantage of the anti-French hysteria to pass a series of laws in 1798 to suppress the Democratic-Republican opposition. The first part of the laws, the Alien Acts, had wide support in the country. These acts increased the time an immigrant must live in America to become a citizen from five to fourteen years. They also allowed the president to deport dangerous aliens or to imprison them during war time.

The Alien Acts were aimed at new immigrants who tended to support the more democratic party of Jefferson. They were also aimed at the hundreds of political refugees who had fled from the law in their own countries to cause trouble in America. The laws were never enforced, but their existence served to encourage many of the worst radicals to leave, and many others decided never to come.

The Sedition Act was aimed squarely at the rights of American citizens to free speech and freedom of the press. It required fines and imprisonment for such "crimes" as publishing any false, scandalous, or malicious statements against the government or organizing to oppose federal laws. This law was used very little, and then exclusively against Democratic-Republican publishers (only ten were convicted).

The Democratic-Republicans obviously led the opposition to the acts. Jefferson and Madison went overboard in opposing them. They succeeded in having the state legislatures in Kentucky and Virginia pass resolutions to **nullify** the laws. The Kentucky and Virginia Resolves were based on the theory that the federal government was a creation of the states, and the states could disallow its laws. Such a position would rob the federal government of all authority over the states. Fortunately, the other states did not join in this extreme position, but it was to be used again in the years leading up to the Civil War. The offensive laws were repealed or allowed to expire over the next two years.

Election of 1800. The election of 1800 was the first that can be described as a fight between

| John Adams was the only Federalist President.

two political parties. Adams faced an uphill battle for re-election. His Federalist Party was divided. The Hamilton wing openly fought against him. The Alien and Sedition Acts had given the Democratic-Republicans an issue to use against the Federalists. Moreover, after all the taxes and preparations, John Adams had not given the country the war they wanted. The well-organized Democratic-Republicans rallied behind Thomas Jefferson and Aaron Burr who ran as a president/vice president team.

The Democratic-Republicans won the election, but the rules for the election caused a serious problem. Each elector was to cast two votes, the one with the most votes became the president, the one in second place became the vice president. The Democratic-Republicans electors loyally cast their two votes, one each for Jefferson and Burr, who therefore tied! A tie was resolved by voting between the candidates in the House of Representatives, which was still under Federalist control. The Federalists supported Burr who was a professional politician, over the idealistic Jefferson. As a result, neither could get the necessary majority in thirty-five consecutive ballots. Finally, Jefferson won on the thirty-sixth when some of the Federalists abstained from voting. (They may have been convinced to do so by Hamilton, who had a strong dislike for Burr). This event brought about the 12th Amendment in 1804 which separated the voting for the two offices.

Federalist legacy. John Adams was the last Federalist president. The party slowly died after that. The divisions within the party hampered its ability to win elections. Its appeal to leadership by the elite did not fit with the growing democratic spirit of the nation. Moreover, once the Democratic-Republicans were in power, they began to support a strong federal government, gaining Federalist supporters as they moved toward Federalist ideas.

However, the Federalists left a rich legacy in America. They set up the basic structure of the national government, established a solid financial system, and protected the new nation from early wars that might have destroyed it. They also established the "loose construction" of the Constitution, giving the new government the flexibility to deal with the changes that were ahead.

 Name the item or person.

1.33 _____	Allowed the president to deport dangerous aliens and increased the time of residency to become a citizen
1.34 _____	Party that won the 1800 elections
1.35 _____	Second president of the United States
1.36 _____	Treaty that triggered a crisis with France
1.37 _____	State resolutions to nullify Alien and Sedition Acts
1.38 _____	Agreement with France under Napoleon that ended the current disputes with America and the alliance
1.39 _____	An attempt by the French government to get bribes for negotiations
1.40 _____	Federalist law that attacked freedom of speech and the press

Answer these questions.

1.41 Who were the two leaders of the Federalist factions?

_____

1.42 What single decision cost John Adams his popularity?

_____

1.43 Publishers with what political party were prosecuted under the Sedition Act?

_____

1.44 What was the rallying cry of the nation preparing for war after the XYZ Affair?

_____

1.45 Who won the electoral vote in 1800?

_____

1.46 Who was Adams' vice president and why was that a problem?

_____

1.47 What was the legacy of the Federalists?

a. _____

b. _____

c. _____

d. _____

Review the material in this section in preparation for the Self Test. The Self Test will check your mastery of this particular section. The items missed on this Self Test will indicate specific areas where restudy is needed for mastery.

SELF TEST 1

Match these people (each answer, 2 points).

1.01 _____ Napoleon Bonaparte

1.02 _____ Alexander Hamilton

1.03 _____ Thomas Jefferson

1.04 _____ George Washington

1.05 _____ John Adams

1.06 _____ Edmond Genêt

1.07 _____ Edmund Randolph

1.08 _____ John Jay

1.09 _____ Aaron Burr

1.010 _____ Henry Knox

a. obtained an unpopular treaty with Britain under President Washington

b. first secretary of state

c. first secretary of the treasury

d. vice presidential candidate who tied with Jefferson in electoral votes in 1800

e. dictator of France

f. troublesome minister from France to America under Washington

g. unanimously chosen president by the electors

h. first and last Federalist president

i. first secretary of war

j. first attorney general

Name the item being described (each answer, 3 points).

1.011 _____ Political party that believed in rule by the elite, a strong central government, and was pro-British

1.012 _____ Political party that believed in rule by the common people, a weak federal government, and was pro-French

1.013 _____ Structure on the reverse of the Great Seal

1.014 _____ A revolt in Pennsylvania in 1794 against the excise tax

1.015 _____ The side that America fought with in the European war that began in 1793

1.016 _____ Scandal that erupted under John Adams when the French demanded a bribe before they would negotiate

1.017 _____ Laws passed by the Federalists to control immigrants and silence opposition to their government

1.018 _____ Agreement between America and France that ended their alliance and settled their current disputes

1.019 _____ The English translation of "E Pluribus Unum"

1.020 _____ Washington's statement that recommended the nation avoid political parties and foreign alliances

Answer these questions (each answer, 4 points).

1.021 What were the three parts of Hamilton's financial plan?

a. _____

b. _____

c. _____

1.022 What was Thomas Jefferson's argument against the National Bank?

_____

1.023 What are three legacies of the Federalist Era?

a. _____

b. _____

c. _____

1.024 What were some of the problems America was having with Britain under Washington?

a. _____

b. _____

c. _____

Answer true or false (each answer, 1 point).

1.025 _____ The national capital was to be built in the south in exchange for a lower tariff rate.

1.026 _____ Alexander Hamilton was vice president under John Adams.

1.027 _____ Citizen Genêt was a British ambassador who negotiated a treaty with the U.S.

1.028 _____ George Washington served two terms as president.

1.029 _____ "Millions for defense but not one cent for tribute" was the rally cry against the British during Washington's term.

1.030 _____ The French and British interfered with American trade.

1.031 _____ Washington did not attach himself to any political party.

1.032 _____ The obverse of the Great Seal has an eagle on it.

1.033 _____ Washington liked politics and eagerly sought the presidency.

1.034 _____ Hamilton favored an agrarian society with a weak federal government.

1.035 _____ John Adams' commitment to peace cost him his popularity.

$\frac{80}{100}$ **SCORE** _____ **TEACHER** _____ _____
initials   date

2. JEFFERSONIAN DEMOCRACY

The election of Thomas Jefferson was a step in the continuing expansion of democracy in America. The old European idea of rule by the elite was slowly being replaced with the idea of rule by the people. Most of the states of the day still would only allow men who owned property to vote, but that was beginning to change. Jefferson was a warm advocate of the common people even though he was clearly a member of the upper class. He was acceptable to the old elites and yet reached out to the growing power of the people.

Jefferson found it impossible to maintain his ideal of a weak federal government when he was in charge. He would repeatedly act in ways not approved by "strict construction" of the Constitution. He justified such actions as being necessary for the "will of the people" and the protection of the country. They also firmly entrenched the idea of a strong, flexible federal government. Ironically, one of the reasons for the continuing decline of the Federalist Party was the fact that many of its supporters became very comfortable with Jefferson's government.

SECTION OBJECTIVES

Review these objectives. When you have completed this section, you should be able to:

1. Describe the important events of the first five presidential administrations.
3. Describe the course and nature of America's problems with Britain that led to the War of 1812.
4. Describe the growth, policies, and decline of the Federalist Party.
5. Describe the growth and policies of the Democratic-Republican Party.
9. Explain the reasons behind U.S. policy decisions from 1789 to the early 1820s.

VOCABULARY

Study these words to enhance your learning success in this section.

arbitrator (är′ bi trā tor). One having the power to make authoritative decisions.

constituent (kon stich′ oo ent). Someone represented by an elected official.

Enlightenment (en līt′ n ment). A philosophical movement of the 18th century, concerned with making a rational re-examination of previously accepted ideas and institutions. It emphasized man's mind as the source of all knowledge and ridiculed faith.

lame duck (lām duk). An elected officeholder or assembly continuing in office during the period between the election of new people and their inauguration.

Democratic-Republicans in Power

Transitions. The election of 1800 was very important in the history of the United States. It was the first time that the ruling party had been defeated in an election. Often in a new republic, the losing party which still has control of the government and the army will use force to keep itself in power. The first change of party power is an important test for any new democracy. America passed that test. The Federalists unhappily but peacefully surrendered power to their political enemies.

Jefferson's election began twenty-five years of Democratic-Republican leadership in America. He immediately set a more informal tone for the presidency. He did not even arrive for his inauguration in a coach. He simply walked over from where he was staying. He shook hands with visitors and sat people at banquets without regard to their rank. He was even known to receive official callers wearing his bathrobe and slippers!

Thomas Jefferson was born into a wealthy Virginia family. He owned large tracts of land in the state and many slaves. He was a brilliant, well-educated man of many interests. He designed his own home, Monticello, near Charlottesville, Virginia, and filled it with many of his own inventions. He had been a member of the Virginia House of Burgesses, a representative at the Continental Congress (where he was the principle author of the Declaration of Independence), an American minister in France, secretary of state and vice president before he was elected to the presidency.

He was a follower of the **Enlightenment** and a "free thinker" where religion was concerned. He was not a Christian. He believed that man's nature was basically good, and by one's own strength evil could be overcome in the world.

Jefferson's policies. In spite of his anti-Federalist rhetoric, Jefferson took a more moderate course once in office. He did not overrule all of the Federalist financial policies. He promised to make full payment on the national debt. The

| The young Washington D.C.

National Bank was left in place as were the tariffs. The excise tax that fell so heavily on Jefferson's beloved farmers was repealed, however.

Jefferson slowly replaced the Federalist office-holders with people from his own party. Although it was done slowly, it was his administration that began the "spoils system" ("to the victor goes the spoils") which allowed government jobs to go to political supporters, rather than qualified workers. Jefferson overturned the Alien and Sedition Acts. The few men convicted under the Sedition Acts were pardoned and their fines returned. The residency requirement for citizenship was brought back down to five years, and the rest of the laws were not renewed when they expired.

Jefferson and his secretary of the treasury, Swiss-born Albert Gallatin, ran the government as cheaply as they could. They took advantage of a lull in the European fighting to vastly reduce the army and navy. They balanced the budget and put as much money as possible into paying off the national debt. In keeping with his philosophy of small government, Jefferson kept the taxes and government expenses low.

Midnight judges. Jefferson proved to be less moderate in dealing with Federalist judges. The **lame duck** Federalist Congress had passed the Judiciary Act of 1801 before the Democratic-Republicans came to power. It created about two hundred new jobs for judges and court officials. John Adams appointed Federalists to these jobs, the Senate quickly approved them, and Adams signed their commissions, (a few even on his last day in office). Rumor stated that some were signed after midnight that night. Jefferson and his party were understandably angered by these "midnight judges" that left the Federalists in power in the judicial branch.

The new Congress repealed the Judiciary Act of 1801, leaving many of the new appointees without jobs to take. Jefferson also ordered that many of the commissions signed by Adams simply not be delivered. One of the appointees, William Marbury, sued Secretary of State James Madison to get his commission. The case was brought in the Supreme Court under an earlier law, the Judiciary Act of 1789.

The chief justice of the Supreme Court was John Marshall, himself a last-minute Federalist appointee. Marshall used *Marbury v. Madison* (1803) to establish the Supreme Court as the final **arbitrator** of the Constitution. He ruled that the Judiciary Act of 1789 was unconstitutional in that it could not require the court to hear these kinds of cases. The Supreme Court was not the right place for Marbury to sue, so it could not make a decision for or against him. Thus Marshall avoided the issue of trying to force an unwilling president to deliver a questionable commission. He also established that the Supreme Court had the power to invalidate a law passed by Congress if it "conflicts" with the Constitution. That power is not given in the Constitution, and it gave the Federalist judiciary tremendous power that would be used more and more as American history progressed.

Jefferson was afraid of how the Federalist judges would use their power and decided to try to remove them. Federal judges were appointed for life under the Constitution and could only be removed by impeachment. Jefferson moved first to impeach John Pickering, a New England judge who was obviously insane.

After he was successfully removed, Jefferson set his sights higher.

In 1804 Jefferson brought impeachment proceedings in the Senate against Samuel Chase, a member of the Supreme Court. Chase was a Federalist judge who openly supported the Federalist agenda on the bench. He had been prominent in the conviction of the Democratic-Republican publishers under the Sedition Act. For impeachment, Jefferson had to prove that Chase was guilty of "high crimes and misdemeanors." The Senators decided that his conduct did not fit that description and acquitted him. Had they convicted him, Jefferson probably would have moved against John Marshall and other judges he did not like. Judges would have had to please the president in order to keep their jobs. The Senate's decision to abide by the plain meaning of the Constitution protected the independence of the federal judges.

Louisiana Purchase. America owned the eastern half of the Mississippi basin. The western half, the Louisiana Territory, was given to Spain after the French and Indian War. In late 1800 Napoleon convinced Spain to return the land to France. This was a dangerous turn of events for America. The west depended upon the Mississippi River and the port of New Orleans for the transport and sale of their products. Spain was an aging power who had agreed to let Americans use both the river and the port. France on the other hand, was an expanding power under Napoleon and might prove difficult to dislodge.

Jefferson acted quickly after he received news of the transfer. He sent James Monroe to France in 1803 to negotiate with the help of Robert Livingston, the American minister there. They were authorized to buy the port of New Orleans and as much land to the east as they could get for a maximum price of ten million dollars. When Monroe reached France he received a staggering surprise. Napoleon, having little success in his schemes in the New World, offered to sell all of Louisiana.

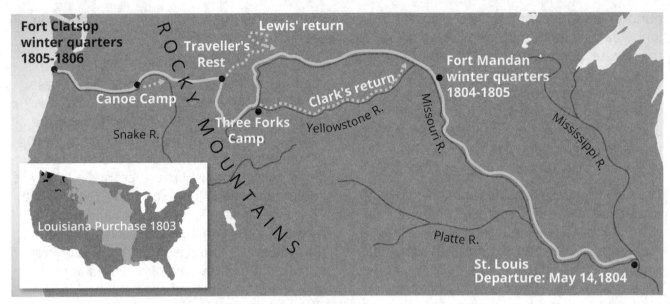

| The Lewis and Clark Expedition 1804-1806 and the Louisiana Purchase

The delegation had no authorization to buy so much land and had no way to contact Jefferson, who was across the Atlantic, for further instructions. The offer was just too good to refuse. Monroe and Livingston negotiated the sale of the land for fifteen million dollars, about three cents an acre.

The treaty put Jefferson in a very difficult position. He did not believe the Constitution authorized him to purchase such a large area of land. He wanted to get an amendment passed to permit it before going forward with the sale. Several of his advisors pointed out that Napoleon might not be willing to wait for that. In the end, the immense advantages of the sale overcame Jefferson's uncertainty. He submitted the treaty to the Senate who rapidly approved it.

The treaty was very popular, especially in the west. It removed the threat of a foreign power on the country's frontier. It guaranteed access to the Mississippi River and gave the country more land for expansion. All or part of fourteen states would eventually be created from the territory. The only losers in the deal were the Federalists, who saw their popularity sink in the light of Jefferson's success.

Lewis and Clark Expedition. The curious Jefferson commissioned a scientific/military expedition to explore and map the new territory. It was led by Jefferson's private secretary, Meriwether Lewis, and frontiersman William Clark, who was the younger brother of Revolutionary War hero George Rogers Clark. They were to try to reach the Pacific Ocean while taking notes on the animals, plants, geographical features, and Native Americans in the land.

The expedition left St. Louis, Missouri in May of 1804. They traveled up the Missouri, across the Rocky Mountains, and down the Columbia River to the Pacific Ocean. They were the first Americans to reach the Pacific overland. A Shoshone woman they met on the way named Sacajawea helped guide them over the mountains. On their return, Lewis and Clark took separate routes to increase the scope of their explorations. They eventually reunited to travel together down the Missouri toward home.

With almost all of their personnel, Lewis and Clark returned to St. Louis in September of 1806. Many people had given them up for dead because they had been gone so long. Their highly successful expedition expanded America's knowledge of the new land. It also gave America a solid claim to the rich Oregon Territory. Meriwether Lewis later became the governor of the very Louisiana Territory that he had explored.

Write true or false.

If the statement is false, change some nouns or adjectives to make it true.

2.1 _____ Jefferson's presidency was less formal than Washington's.

2.2 _____ The right of the Supreme Court to determine if laws are constitutional was set by *Marbury v. Marshall* in 1803.

2.3 _____ Thomas Jefferson brought impeachment proceedings against John Marshall in 1804.

2.4 _____ Thomas Jefferson reduced the army and navy when he was president.

2.5 _____ The treaty to purchase Louisiana was very unpopular.

2.6 _____ Lewis and Clark were the first Americans to reach the Pacific Ocean overland.

2.7 _____ Lewis and Clark traveled in the west for about a year.

2.8 _____ Pocahontas was a woman who helped Lewis and Clark.

2.9 _____ Jefferson's home in Virginia was Monticello.

Answer these questions.

2.10 Why was the election of 1800 important in the development of the American republic?

_____

_____

2.11 What (if anything) did Jefferson change in the Federalist finance system?

_____

2.12 Why were Americans concerned about France taking over Louisiana?

_____

_____

_____

2.13 What did Jefferson do about the Alien and Sedition Acts?

_____

_____

2.14 What was the financial and tax policy of Jefferson and Gallatin?

_____

_____

2.15 What did Jefferson believe he needed before he could accept the Louisiana Purchase?

_____

2.16 What route did Lewis and Clark follow to the Pacific?

_____

_____

Problems and Controversies

The Shores of Tripoli. The nations of the north coast of Africa (called the Barbary Coast) made a rich living attacking the ships that sailed in the Mediterranean. These pirates had routinely been paid off by the major trading nations to leave their ships alone. Jefferson objected to paying bribes and ransom (for captured sailors). He had long argued that the military should fight the pirates, not pay them.

The Pasha of Tripoli gave Jefferson his chance, when he declared war on the U.S. in 1801 because he was unhappy with his share of the tribute. Jefferson dispatched the reduced American navy to deal with the pirates more forcefully. The navy and the marines successfully fought a four-year war with the pirates, earning experience and international respect. (The marines immortalized the battles by including the "shores of Tripoli" in their hymn). Eventually, the Americans won a treaty with reduced payments. After a few years of fighting, the payments were stopped entirely.

Burr Conspiracy. Some New England Federalists were concerned that new states created in the Louisiana Territory would eliminate their influence in the federal government. They hatched a plot to take New England, New York and New Jersey out of the Union. They were joined in the plot by the Democratic-Republican vice president Aaron Burr who was out of favor with Jefferson. Burr ran for governor of New York in 1804, intending to use the office to support the plot. He was defeated with the help of Alexander Hamilton.

After the election, Burr challenged Hamilton to a duel and killed him. That incident ended Burr's political career and further depleted the Federalist Party. Burr fled to Pennsylvania after New York and New Jersey charged him with murder. In New York, he hatched a plot to invade Spanish territory, and possibly set up a separate government in the west. He organized a group of armed men and headed down the Ohio River. It is uncertain exactly what he intended to do, but one of his fellow conspirators, James Wilkinson, decided to back out and informed Jefferson of their actions.

Jefferson had Burr arrested and put on trial for treason in May of 1807. John Marshall was the judge at the trial which was held in Virginia. The Constitution requires two witnesses to convict someone of treason. Marshall interpreted it to mean that there had to be two witnesses to each separate act of treason. That was not possible and, in any case, the evidence was very confused. Much to Jefferson's disgust, Burr was acquitted. The stigma of the death of Hamilton and his trial led him to withdraw to Europe. He was never again politically active in America.

Growing problems with Britain. The country was so prosperous that Jefferson was overwhelmingly re-elected in 1804. However, there were dangerous clouds on the national horizon. Immediately after the sale of Louisiana, Napoleon declared war on Britain. In 1805 he defeated the Austrian and Russian armies in Austria at Austerlitz. Earlier that same year, Britain had destroyed the French fleet at Trafalgar, south of Spain. The combination of the two victories left France in control of Europe and Britain in control of the oceans.

The two sides were secure in their own areas and could not directly fight each other. So both began a campaign to starve each other into submission. Napoleon used his control of Europe to cut off its trade with Britain and Britain used its control of the seas to cut off all other trade with the entire continent. In 1806 and 1807 Britain issued Orders in Council (an order from the king on the advice of his council) that all neutral ships found on the sea sailing near French-controlled lands were to be seized. Such ships must stop first in Britain to have their cargo examined. France in turn ordered all ships that stopped in Britain to be seized if they came to France. American trade fell as both sides took ships and cargoes.

The British stepped up their impressment of sailors in a desperate attempt to keep their hard-pressed navy at full strength. Life in the British navy was incredibly harsh and inhumane. Many British sailors had deserted, obtained legal or fraudulent American citizenship, and had began serving on American ships for better pay and better conditions. It was these Englishmen that the British were "officially" after when they searched American merchant ships. They would claim that a man born English is always English. In fact, the British captains took many men who had never even been English, without any rebuke from London. The American navy had been so reduced under Jefferson that there was no way it could protect U.S. shipping and the British clearly knew this.

The contempt the British held for American rights was illustrated by the *Chesapeake-Leopard* affair in 1807. The American warship *Chesapeake* was approached by the British ship *Leopard* a few miles off the coast of Virginia. The British captain demanded the surrender of four deserters he claimed were aboard the American ship. Even though his guns were not ready, the

| The *Leopard* attacking the *Chesapeake*

American captain refused. The British opened fire, killing three men, injuring eighteen, and badly damaging the ship. The Americans surrendered, the British took the four men, and the Chesapeake limped back to port.

The British captain clearly exceeded his government's guidelines by attacking a neutral warship, but the British government was reluctant to admit error and refused the American demand to give up impressment. The American public cried out for war. Jefferson did not want one. America's small, poorly equipped army and navy proved the nation was not ready. Jefferson searched for an honorable alternative.

Embargo disaster. Jefferson decided to force the European powers to respect American rights by cutting off trade with them. He hoped that they needed American supplies badly enough that they would meet his demands. Congress passed Jefferson's Embargo Act in 1807. It forbade the export of any American goods on any ship. It was a long way from Jefferson's earlier position under Washington that the federal government did not even have the power to charter a bank!

The Embargo Act was an unqualified disaster. Legitimate trade came to a halt. The docks of the American port cities were deserted.

Thousands lost their jobs in the shipping, storage, exchange, and shipbuilding industries. Crops such as cotton, grain, and tobacco that supplied cash for western and southern farmers could not be sold abroad. The entire country suffered from the crisis. Napoleon added a humiliating note to the law when he began to "enforce" it in Europe by seizing any American vessels that happened to reach port there.

The embargo quickly raised a storm of opposition. Angry citizens called it the "O Grab Me" (embargo spelled backwards). A flourishing illegal trade grew along the U.S.-Canadian border. The New England states, which were the most dependent on trade, talked of leaving the Union. Jefferson's popularity plummeted, especially after he convinced Congress to pass tough laws to enforce the embargo.

The embargo also failed to cause any real harm to Britain. The British had good crops that year—enough to meet their food requirements. Some of the depleted trade was taken up by the new republics in South America. The English were not willing to consider any American demands to restore trade. Jefferson finally admitted defeat and signed the repeal of the law days before he left office. It had been in effect for fourteen months.

 Complete these sentences.

2.17 Aaron Burr killed _____ in a duel.

2.18 The French land victory at _____ and the British sea victory at _____ created a stalemate in the European war.

2.19 Aaron Burr was acquitted on the charge of _____ in 1807.

2.20 The British ship _____ attacked the American ship _____ in 1807 to recover four deserters; in the process the British killed three Americans and injured eighteen.

2.21 America fought a four year war with the pirates along the north coast of _____ under Thomas Jefferson.

2.22 Jefferson tried to deal with European interference with American ships by the _____ Act of 1807.

2.23 Aaron Burr's conspiracy was exposed by _____ , a co-conspirator who decided to back out.

2.24 British issued _____ in 1806 and 1807 that ordered their navy to seize all neutral ships headed for French-held Europe.

2.25 The British tried to keep their ships at full staff by the _____ of sailors on American ships.

2.26 Jefferson signed the _____ of the Embargo Act right before he left office.

HISTORY & GEOGRAPHY 804

LIFEPAC TEST

NAME _____

DATE _____

SCORE _____

HISTORY & GEOGRAPHY 804: LIFEPAC TEST

Put a _C_ beside items that were a cause of the War of 1812, an _R_ beside those that were results of the war, and a _P_ beside those that were attempts to prevent war (each answer, 2 points).

1. _____ Embargo Act

2. _____ Impressment

3. _____ Nationalism

4. _____ Rise of American Manufacturing

5. _____ British support of Tecumseh

6. _____ Jay's Treaty

7. _____ _Chesapeake-Leopard_ Affair

8. _____ Improvement in British-American relations

9. _____ Eliminated the Native American resistance on the frontier

10. _____ Orders in Council

Name the item described (each answer, 3 points).

11. _____ State ceded by Spain after Andrew Jackson defeated the Seminole Indians there

12. _____ Scandal under John Adams when the French would not negotiate without a bribe

13. _____ Political party that set up the basic government structure, a solid financial system and "loose construction"

14. _____ The obverse has an eagle holding an olive branch and thirteen arrows, the reverse has a pyramid

15. _____ western Mississippi land purchased by Jefferson in spite of his belief it was unconstitutional

16. _____ Laws passed by the Federalist Party to control immigrants and silence opposition to the government

17. _____ Revenue for transportation was to come from these under Henry Clay's American System

18. _____ Name for the time under the Monroe administration when the country was united and content

19. _____   Fort that was successfully defended in the Battle of Baltimore

20. _____   Federalist group that wanted to weaken the federal government near the end of the War of 1812

Match these people (each answer, 2 points).

21. _____ John Marshall   a. hero of the Battle of New Orleans

22. _____ Tecumseh   b. first secretary of war

23. _____ Henry Clay   c. first leader of Democratic-Republicans

24. _____ Oliver Perry   d. Battle of Lake Erie

25. _____ Alexander Hamilton   e. Anti-American Confederacy organizer

26. _____ Henry Knox   f. president; asked for war with Britain

27. _____ Andrew Jackson   g. Speaker of the House; War Hawk

28. _____ Thomas Jefferson   h. Federalist chief justice; Supreme Court

29. _____ James Madison   i. first secretary of the treasury

30. _____ James Monroe   j. president; warned Europe not to interfere in America

Choose the best answer (each answer, 3 points).

31. Thomas Jefferson opposed the National Bank because _____ .
     a. it would take capital from state banks
     b. it was not specifically permitted by the Constitution
     c. it would benefit mainly rich investors
     d. he was afraid of the power it would have

32. The most important issue facing Washington's administration was _____ .
     a. the Whiskey Rebellion
     b. British occupation of forts in the Old Northwest
     c. finances
     d. where to locate the capital

33. The Federalists declined as a political party because _____ .
     a. the Democratic-Republicans took over much of their agenda
     b. most of their support was in New England
     c. John Adams was unpopular
     d. Alexander Hamilton was killed in a duel

34. The significance of the election of 1800 was that _____ .
     a. Adams did not win a second term
     b. Jefferson introduced a more relaxed style of government
     c. the Federalists never won the presidency again
     d. there was a peaceful change in political power

35. The Treaty of Ghent did not cost America any territory because _____ .
    a. of the Battle of New Orleans
    b. Britain was exhausted from twenty years of war
    c. the British did not get the victories they expected
    d. Napoleon was threatening Europe again

36. America entered the War of 1812 at a disadvantage because _____ .
    a. New England opposed the war
    b. the army and navy were inadequate
    c. the National Bank was no longer in existence
    d. France was still seizing American ships

37. The goal of the U.S. in the War of 1812 was _____ .
    a. to capture Canada
    b. to end years of mistreatment by the British
    c. to force free trade
    d. prove the worth of her navy

38. New England opposed the War of 1812 because _____ .
    a. they opposed Madison
    b. it stopped trade
    c. they did not want Canadian land to add more states
    d. it stopped tariff revenue

39. Thomas Jefferson tried to impeach several judges because _____ .
    a. they were incompetent
    b. they were appointed by the lame duck Federalists
    c. he was afraid of the power of lifetime-appointed Federalist judges
    d. he wanted to expand the spoils system

40. Washington's greatest success as president was _____ .
    a. putting down the Whiskey Rebellion
    b. providing the nation with the early stability it needed
    c. choosing the best men for his cabinet
    d. establishing the First National Bank

✎ **Answer these questions.**

2.27 Did the embargo accomplish its purpose? _____

Explain. _____

_____

2.28 What caused the war with the Barbary pirates?

_____

_____

2.29 How did Americans react to the embargo?

_____

_____

2.30 What plot was Aaron Burr involved with when he ran for governor of New York?

_____

_____

War Hawks

Elections of 1808 and 1810. Thomas Jefferson decided not to run for another term as president. He was afraid that the men who followed him might try to keep the office for life. So like Washington before him, he served only two terms. He retired to Monticello, helped found the University of Virginia, and renewed his broken friendship with John Adams who was living in retirement in Massachusetts. The two old friends and revolutionaries carried on a lively correspondence in their declining years. By a memorable act of Providence, John Adams and Thomas Jefferson both died on July 4, 1826, the fiftieth anniversary of the Declaration of Independence.

Thomas Jefferson was not active in the election of 1808, but he was pleased when his good friend and secretary of state, James Madison, was elected president. Madison defeated the Federalist candidate, C. C. Pinckney by more than a two-to-one margin in the electoral votes. With their pro-British agenda and New England power base, the Federalists were declining rapidly as more western states were added and anti-British sentiment grew.

The growing anger against Britain and the natural passage of time brought significant changes in Congress, most noticeably in the House of Representatives. In 1808 and particularly in 1810, a new crop of Representatives came to dominate the House. They were young men, often from the west. They had not fought or served in the Revolution. They had no first-hand experience of what the high cost of a war with Great Britain would be. They were eager to defend their nation's honor and expand her borders. History named them the "War Hawks."

War Hawks. The leader of the War Hawks was a young man who would be prominent in American politics for many decades. His name was Henry Clay. Clay was a brilliant speaker from Kentucky who was chosen as Speaker of the House in 1811. He used that position to appoint War Hawks to head important committees and dominate the House. Another member of the Hawks was John Calhoun of South Carolina. Calhoun also would be prominent on the American political stage for several decades to come.

The War Hawks were primarily from the west and the south. They were avidly in favor of war with Britain. They were men who had known no other country but the United States and were passionately nationalistic. They wanted to capture Canada and naively believed it would be a simple matter, since Britain was busy fighting in Europe. They also hoped to take Florida from Spain. The farmers from their states badly needed free trade in order to sell their goods abroad. The War Hawks' **constituents** also wanted to rid the frontier of attacks lead by Native Americans.

Tecumseh's Confederacy. One of the most remarkable leaders of the Native Americans resistance to the American pioneer flood was Tecumseh, a Shawnee leader from the Ohio country. He was a skilled orator who succeeded in organizing Native American people from all over the eastern Mississippi basin into an anti-American confederacy. He was assisted by his brother, "the Prophet," who claimed to have had a revelation and led a spiritual organization of the tribes.

In 1811 General William Henry Harrison led an American army to drive the confederation out of lands they had given away by treaty. Harrison was attacked by the Prophet not far from Tecumseh's headquarters at Tippecanoe.

| Henry Clay, Champion of the War Hawks

Harrison defeated the Native Americans and burned their settlement. He also found a large supply of British guns and powder in the settlement.

The defeat broke the power of the Prophet and dispersed the confederacy. Still, Tecumseh convinced many of the tribes to fight with the British during the upcoming War of 1812. He was killed in 1813 at the battle of the Thames in Canada.

The slide toward War. News of British supplies in the hands of the Native Americans further inflamed the War Hawks. They believed Britain was aiding and plotting with Tecumseh's Confederacy. They pushed ever harder for a war with Britain.

The situation was extremely difficult to resolve. Britain was fighting, possibly for its own survival, against one of the greatest dictators in history. Napoleon had conquered most of Europe, putting his family and friends on the thrones of its nations. Now he was looking for new lands to conquer. Britain was almost alone in trying to stop him. Meanwhile, America wanted to make wartime profits in trade without choosing sides. Britain was in no mood to compromise and neither were the War Hawks.

President Madison had searched desperately for a way to avoid a war. The Embargo Act was replaced in 1809 by the Non-Intercourse Act, which allowed trade with any nation except Britain or France. This was replaced in 1810 by Macon's Bill No. 2. This law allowed trade with all nations, but included what Congress hoped would be a enticing lure. If Britain or France would repeal their orders to capture U.S. ships, America would stop trading with their opponent.

Napoleon seized on this new law as a way to restore the American trade embargo against Britain. He publicly announced in November of 1810 that he would no longer seize American ships. Madison foolishly believed him and ordered all trade with Britain to be stopped. In fact, the French never had recalled their orders and continued to capture American ships. Britain demanded proof of the French decision and continued her own seizures. Relations between America and the former mother country continued to deteriorate.

War. America was totally unprepared for war. Jefferson had left the nation without a substantial navy or army. The War Hawks foolishly believed the war would be fought on land in Canada and refused to improve the navy in the time leading up to the war. Even when Congress did increase the size of the army, they were not able to overcome the lack of organization and trained officers. The army would have to rely on additions from the state militia, and many people felt the militia could not legally fight outside the United States. In fact, many of the militia refused to fight in Canada, which further undermined the military situation.

The nation's financial situation added to the military problems. The Democratic-Republicans had allowed the Charter for the hated National Bank to expire in 1811, leaving the nation without any central financial structure. Embargoes and trade problems had cut off the government's income from tariffs. The Democratic-Republicans, true to their Jeffersonian origins, opposed internal taxes needed to prepare for war. They finally agreed to them once war was already declared, which cut off any hope of having a nation ready in advance.

The hard realities of the situation did not disturb the well-organized War Hawks. They continued to press for war, confident that a simple invasion of Canada would force Britain to come to terms. Madison finally gave in to his own frustrations, pressure from the War Hawks, and the temptation of capturing Canada. He asked Congress to declare war in June of 1812. In support of the request, he sent a list of grievances, which included impressment, the seizure of American ships and British support of Native American attacks on Americans. Congress voted in favor of war on June 17th and 18th. The war Washington, Adams, and Jefferson avoided had finally arrived.

Complete the following.

2.31 Who won the presidential election of 1808? _____

2.32 Name two young War Hawks that would be important political leaders for decades.

_____

2.33 Who was the American commander at the Battle of Tippecanoe?

_____

2.34 Name four of the reasons why the War Hawks favored war.

a. _____

b. _____

c. _____

d. _____

2.35 What was significant about the day Adams and Jefferson died?

_____

2.36 What did Tecumseh do that threatened the U.S. frontier?

_____

_____

2.37 Give five reasons why the U.S. was not prepared for war.

a. _____

b. _____

c. _____

d. _____

e. _____

2.38 What part of the country did the War Hawks come from?

_____

2.39 Why did the Battle of Tippecanoe increase American hostility toward Britain?

_____

2.40 Why was it significant that most of the War Hawks were young?

_____

_____

2.41 What territory did the War Hawks expect to capture easily? _____

2.42 What trick did Napoleon play on Madison in regard to Macon's Bill No. 2?

_____

_____

2.43 What month and year did America declare war on Britain?

_____

2.44 What were the reasons given by President Madison for declaring war?

a. _____

b. _____

c. _____

↺ **Review the material in this section in preparation for the Self Test.** This Self Test will check your mastery of this particular section as well as your knowledge of the previous section.

SELF TEST 2

Name the item described (each answer, 3 points).

2.01 _____ Scandal under John Adams over an attempt by French official to demand bribes before negotiation

2.02 _____ Young representatives from the west and south, elected in 1808 and 1810, who favored war with Great Britain

2.03 _____ A revolt in Pennsylvania during George Washington's presidency against the excise tax

2.04 _____ Laws passed by the Federalists to control recent immigrants and restrict the free speech of Democratic-Republican publishers

2.05 _____ Land purchased from France in 1803 for 3 cents an acre that Jefferson was not sure he could constitutionally take

2.06 _____ Expedition to explore the land purchased from France; men were the first Americans to reach the Pacific Ocean by an overland route

2.07 _____ Political party of John Adams

2.08 _____ Political party of Thomas Jefferson

2.09 _____ Supreme Court decision that created the right of the court to invalidate a law passed by Congress as unconstitutional

2.010 _____ The disastrous law passed under Jefferson to cut off trade and force the European nations to honor U.S. neutrality

Answer these questions (each answer, 4 points).

2.011 What were three grievances America had against Britain under Washington that were named as reasons for the War of 1812?

a. _____

b. _____

c. _____

2.012 Did Jefferson follow "strict construction" after he became president? _____

Give an example. _____

_____

2.013 What was the *Chesapeake-Leopard* incident of 1807?

_____

_____

2.014 Name three legacies of the Federalist Era.

a. _____

b. _____

c. _____

2.015 What was the significance in American history of the election of 1800?

_____

2.016 What "war" was fought during Jefferson's administration?

_____

Match these people (each answer, 2 points).

2.017 _____ Thomas Jefferson

2.018 _____ George Washington

2.019 _____ John Calhoun

2.020 _____ John Marshall

2.021 _____ Sacajawea

2.022 _____ Aaron Burr

2.023 _____ Napoleon

2.024 _____ James Madison

2.025 _____ Tecumseh

2.026 _____ Henry Clay

a. Alexander Hamilton set his financial policies

b. Shoshone woman who aided Lewis and Clark

c. chief justice of the Supreme Court

d. representative from Kentucky; Speaker of the House

e. organized the Native Americans of the eastern Mississippi into an anti-American alliance

f. representative from South Carolina

g. third president of the U.S.

h. dictator of France

i. president who finally asked for war with Britain

j. led a conspiracy that possibly intended to create a new government in the west

Choose the letters of the correct answers (1 point for each letter, chosen or not).

2.027 Which of the following were part of the controversy between Jefferson and the Federalist judiciary? _____
  a. Many were appointed after the election of 1800 under the Judiciary Act of 1801, which was also passed after the election.
  b. The appointments, approval, and commissioning of the judges were hurried through procedures by the Federalists after the election of 1800.
  c. Jefferson was able to successfully use impeachment to get rid of the Federalist judges he opposed.
  d. The Democratic-Republican Congress used the Judiciary Act of 1801 to appoint their own judges to the bench.

2.028 Each of the following either moved America and Britain closer to war or were used to avoid it.

  Choose the ones that moved the nations toward war. _____
  a. Orders in Council
  b. Non-Intercourse Act
  c. Jay's Treaty
  d. Austerlitz and Trafalgar
  e. Tecumseh's Confederacy
  f. Washington's Farewell Address

80
/100   SCORE _____   TEACHER _____ _____
                                              initials   date

3. WAR OF 1812

The War of 1812 has been called the Second War for Independence, because it established America's reputation as a nation. Britain began acting like a bully by meddling in the Northwest Territory and disregarded America's rights on the open sea. The Americans stood up to the bully in the War of 1812. This time, the Americans fought alone, without any European allies. Britain could not blame American victories on the French. The war established a new respect for America and its armed forces, particularly the navy.

This was a war that began and ended with irony. The Orders in Council, a major cause of the war, were withdrawn days before war was declared because the drop in trade was hurting British merchants. The greatest American victory, the Battle of New Orleans, was fought after the peace treaty was signed that ended the war.

Those ironic twists almost perfectly describe this bumbling war. The Americans were unable to capture Canada, as they so arrogantly believed they could. The tiny American navy astounded the British by besting many of her warships in one-on-one battle. At one point, the British tried to dictate terms for peace, only to find that the Americans were doing much better than they had thought. It was a war of confusion that was fought in a series of small, scattered battles which ended in a draw. The war was ended by a treaty that was essentially a cease-fire agreement.

SECTION OBJECTIVES

Review these objectives. When you have completed this section, you should be able to:

1. Describe the important events of the first five presidential administrations.
2. Describe the growth, policies, and decline of the Federalist Party.
3. Describe the growth and policies of the Democratic-Republican Party.
4. Describe the course and results of the War of 1812.
5. Describe how America changed after the War of 1812.
6. Describe the development of the power of the Supreme Court under John Marshall.
7. Explain the reasons behind U.S. policy decisions from 1789 to the early 1820s.

VOCABULARY

Study these words to enhance your learning success in this section.

annex (a neks'). To incorporate territory into an existing country.

arbitration (är' bi trā shun). The process by which the parties to a dispute submit their differences to the judgment of an impartial party appointed by mutual consent.

czar (zär). A king or emperor; especially one of the former emperors of Russia.

depression (di presh' en). A period of drastic decline in the national economy characterized by decreasing business activity, falling prices, and unemployment.

frigate (frig' it). A high speed, medium-sized sailing warship of the 17th-19th century.

nationalism (nash' un ul iz' em). Devotion to the interests of a particular nation.

speculate (spek' yu lāt). To engage in the buying or selling of a commodity with an element of risk on the chance of great profit.

status quo (stā' tus kwō). The existing condition or state of affairs.

Not the War They Planned

New England. New England bitterly opposed the War of 1812. It was often referred to there as "Mr. Madison's War." This region was the last stronghold of the pro-British Federalists. They believed that America should be helping Britain to defeat the despot Napoleon, not help him in defeating Britain! New England was also the center of American trade, which was mainly trade with Great Britain. The profits were so high in wartime that New England merchants continued to make money, even if only a few of their ships ran all the blockades. The war stopped the profits. Some of the New Englanders went so far as to support the British with loans and supplies during the war! The American war effort was handicapped by disunity in the nation.

Invasion of Canada. The mainspring of the American plan, the invasion of Canada, was a disaster. The American strategy called for a three-way invasion: from Detroit and Niagara, between the Great Lakes, and up Lake Champlain to Montreal. The Americans believed the Canadian people would not put up much of a fight for faraway Britain, especially since most of them were French. Instead, the Canadians fought bravely and fiercely—they were defending their homes against an alien invader. Many Canadians were former Americans who had been loyal to Britain during the Revolution. Forced to flee when threatened in America, they fought valiantly to prevent their new land from also falling to the Revolutionaries.

The attack from Detroit was under the command of General William Hull. Hull had been an officer in the Revolution but was now old and unsure of himself. He led an army into Canada but quickly retreated because of fears about his supply lines. The British commander, Isaac

Brock, took advantage of Hull's hesitation and marched his army toward Detroit. Brock threatened that if he captured the city, he might not be able to control his Native American allies.

Fearful of such a result, Hull surrendered without firing a single shot. In August of 1812, Hull surrendered to a force that was much smaller than his own! He was later court-martialed and condemned to death but was pardoned by Madison for his services during the Revolution. His cowardice cost America control of the Detroit region.

General Stephen Van Rensselaer led the American attack from Niagara. His small army ran into stiff British resistance and was defeated when the militia reinforcements refused to cross the border. The militiamen stayed on the American side while the British killed their countrymen across the river. General Henry Dearborn, who commanded the attack toward Montreal, withdrew without seriously engaging the enemy when the militia under his command refused to leave the country. Meanwhile, the British and their Native American allies captured Fort Michilimackinac between Lake Huron and Lake Superior in July of 1812. The Canadian campaign of 1812 was a complete failure.

Naval War. The fiasco of the Canadian adventure was partially redeemed by the surprising American success at sea. The American **frigates** succeeded in defeating and capturing several of their British counterparts. This was a humiliating turn for the proud British navy and a boost for American morale.

The most famous American frigate, the *U.S.S. Constitution*, defeated and captured the *H.M.S. Guerriére* in August of 1812. The American

| Oliver Hazard Perry transferring his command over to the *Niagara*.

vessel, under the command of Isaac Hull, the nephew of disgraced William Hull, had more guns and a larger crew than its opponent. Moreover, British cannon fire bounced off the heavy oak sides of the *Constitution*, earning it the affectionate nickname "Old Ironsides."

The success of the *Constitution* was quickly followed by others. The *United States* under Stephen Decatur, a naval hero from the war against the Barbary pirates, captured the British frigate *Macedonian*. The *U.S.S. Wasp* defeated the *Frolic*, the *Essex* captured the *Alert,* and the *Hornet* took the *H.M.S. Peacock*. In October of 1812, the *Constitution* struck again under a new commander, William Bainbridge, and sunk the *Java*. The U.S. also suffered a loss in June of 1813 when the British frigate *Shannon* defeated the smaller *Chesapeake* (which had been so humiliated in the *Chesapeake-Leopard* Affair of 1807). Overall, the single ship combat tended to go to the Americans with thirteen wins to the British three.

The few losses did not seriously threaten the huge British navy, but it did humiliate them. Their navy commanders had mocked the

Americans at the beginning of the war. Their overconfidence was badly misplaced. The American frigates were heavier, had larger crews, and carried more firepower than the British ships. American ships were all manned by patriots who were defending their nation's honor, not by poor, luckless men forced into service as with the British. The British finally ordered their frigates to sail in pairs to avoid any more single ship battles.

The naval campaign also included about five hundred American privateers. These were smaller, quicker ships that attacked and captured British merchant vessels for profit. They captured over a thousand ships during the war, some of them from the Irish Sea and the English Channel. These losses further angered the British government and a public already stung by the loss of the frigates. The English business class turned against the war as their losses mounted.

Canadian Campaign of 1813. Command of the troubled front at Detroit was given to William Henry Harrison, the hero of Tippecanoe. He quickly determined that he could not retake Detroit without having control of the Great Lakes. The lakes were the key for both transportation and communication along the U.S.-Canadian border. Captain Oliver Hazard Perry was given the task of gaining control of the waterways.

Perry's first job was to obtain a fleet. At Presque Isle on Lake Erie he spent the summer of 1813 building five ships. Five more were towed by oxen up the rapids of the Niagara River from Lake Ontario. In September Perry sailed his fleet to the western end of Lake Erie and met the British.

The Battle of Lake Erie was incredibly fierce. Perry's flagship, the *Lawrence,* was destroyed. He moved his command to the *Niagara* which broke through the British line, firing at them from both sides as it passed. The British were defeated, and the lake came under American control. "We have met the enemy and they are ours," Perry reported back to Washington. The victory was a sweet balm to America's shattered cause in the north.

The British withdrew from Detroit once they realized they could not hold it without support from the water. They retreated eastward and were met at the Thames River in Canada by Harrison and over three thousand American troops. The outnumbered British (with their Native American allies) were quickly defeated. The Americans thus regained control of the Detroit region. The great organizer, Tecumseh, was killed, which destroyed his confederacy and ended the Native American alliance with the British.

The campaign of 1813 had undone some of the damage of the previous year's fiasco, but Canada and the far northwest American frontier were still in British hands. A second attempt by the Americans under James Wilkinson and Wade Hampton to capture Montreal failed in 1813. The British succeeded in capturing Fort Niagara and burning the city of Buffalo, New York in that same year. The Canadian front was reduced to a stalemate for the remainder of the war.

Match these people.

3.1	_____ William Hull	a. victor at the Battle of the Thames
3.2	_____ William Bainbridge	b. British commander in Canada
3. 3	_____ Oliver Perry	c. victor at the Battle of Lake Erie
3.4	_____ Isaac Brock	d. *Constitution* commander, captured the *Guerriere*
3.5	_____ Stephen Decatur	
3.6	_____ Henry Dearborn	e. commander of the *United States*, hero of Barbary Coast war
3.7	_____ Stephen Van Rensselaer	
3.8	_____ William Henry Harrison	f. *Constitution* commander, sunk the *Java*
3.9	_____ Isaac Hull	g. cowardly officer who surrendered Detroit
		h. failed in march on Montreal
		i. lost battle in attack from *Niagara* because the militia would not leave the country

Write the correct answer.

3.10 What bitter New Englanders named the war _____

3.11 Fort between Lakes Huron and Superior _____

3.12 Nickname of the *Constitution* _____

3.13 Message Perry sent after his victory _____

_____

3.14 Small, quick, American ships that captured over 1,000 British merchantmen for profit

_____

Answer these questions.

3.15 Why did New England oppose the War of 1812?

a. _____

b. _____

3.16 What did America primarily want to capture in the War of 1812? _____

3.17 Why did the American ships fare so well against the British in one-on-one ship battles?

_____

_____

3.18 Where did Captain Perry get his fleet?

_____

_____

To the Depths of Despair and Back

In 1814 events in Europe took an ominous turn against the Americans. In October 1813, Napoleon was seriously defeated in the Battle of the Nations at Leipzig. The loss forced him to abdicate in April of 1814 and exile himself to the Mediterranean island of Elba. That freed Britain to concentrate its massive military strength on America. By the spring of 1814, experienced, battle-hardened British officers and soldiers who had just won a great victory in Europe were now taking up positions in the New World.

Last attempt at Canada. In 1814 the Americans made one last attempt to invade Canada under the leadership of Generals Jacob Brown and Winfield Scott. These commanders led an army across the Niagara River and defeated the British at the Battle of Chippewa in July. The troops coming from Europe began adding their weight to the fray. Later that same month, the Americans were driven back at the Battle of Lundy's Lane. The Americans held the British at Fort Erie for several months and then withdrew, ending the last American attempt to bring Canada into the Union by force.

British strategy. The British ended the string of American naval victories by establishing a tight blockade all along the east coast. The blockade ruined the remainder of American trade and cut off all tariff revenue for the government. By the end of the war the nation's economy was in a shambles, and the government was almost bankrupt.

The British strategy was to inflict several large defeats on the Americans and force them to sign away large chunks of territory in exchange for peace. An army of over 10,000 was assembled in Canada for an invasion of New York along the traditional route down Lake Champlain. Another was assembled in the West Indies to move against New Orleans.

The British also used their control of the seas to land troops along the American coastline. Much of eastern Maine was captured. Several of the towns along the coast were plundered by the roving British navy, but with troops freed by the defeat of Napoleon, the British moved for bigger prizes.

The burning of Washington. The British fleet under Admiral George Cockburn had taken complete control of Chesapeake Bay in the summer of 1814. He and British general Robert Ross led an attack against the American capital in August. The Americans had not expected an attack there and had only slight defenses. The British disembarked without any resistance in Maryland and marched toward Washington. A hastily assembled militia force met them at the Battle of Bladensburg. The Americans quickly fled from the professional British army which marched into the capital unopposed.

Most of the population of the city fled before the British arrived. Government clerks had hidden or removed important papers. President Madison rode down to the front and fled with the retreating army. His wife Dolley Madison had been at the president's mansion all day packing up valuable goods and papers to take with her. She stayed until late in the afternoon, even when cannon fire could be heard in the distance. One of the last items she took out was the priceless painting of George Washington by Gilbert Stuart. She had the frame broken so the canvas could be moved easily. At last she also fled. Washington was almost deserted when the British arrived on the night of August 24, 1814.

The British burned most of the public buildings in Washington, including the capital and the president's house. They also burned the offices of the local newspaper. A huge thunderstorm put out most of the fires that night and contained the damage. The British withdrew to their ships, fearing that an American army was assembling to face them. The president's mansion was completely gutted by the fire. It was eventually repaired and the outside whitewashed to cover the black marks of the fire. It became known as the White House from then on.

Negotiations in Europe. Russia was a British ally in the war against Napoleon. The Russian czar sent a peace feeler in 1814, which resulted in British-American negotiations in Ghent, Belgium. The American delegation was led by future president John Quincy Adams, the son of John Adams. Henry Clay was also a delegate. The war was running very much in favor of the British when the two sides met for the first time.

The British negotiators made sweeping demands based on their confidence that the Americans

| The burning of the President's Mansion

were losing the war. The facts supported their view. Britain occupied parts of Maine and the upper Mississippi basin. A British army was moving down Lake Champlain, and another was organizing in the West Indies. The American capital had been sacked without any serious resistance. The British felt quite secure in dictating terms to their American counterparts.

The British demanded an independent Native American nation created out of the land west of the Mississippi, south of the Great Lakes. They also demanded permanent control of the Great Lakes, and a large part of land in Maine. The American delegation refused without even bothering to send the offer back to Madison for his decision. Both sides then waited for further developments in America. This was the low point of the war for the tattered United States. Things were about to improve.

Battle of Plattsburgh Bay. In the summer of 1814, the British advanced along the traditional Canadian-American invasion route, Lake Champlain. The British had to maintain control of the lake in order to move their supplies. The British fleet supporting the invasion was met by a weaker American force at Plattsburgh Bay in September. Once again, the balance of the war hung on a naval battle on an inland lake. The Americans under the command of Thomas Macdonough fought a desperate, bloody battle that ended in their favor. With supply and communication lines cut off by the American control of Lake Champlain, the British retreated.

Baltimore. Americans were infuriated by the attack on their capital. When Cockburn and Ross moved to attack the privateer center of Baltimore in September they met an angry, prepared enemy. The British attacked by both land and sea. The land attack was quickly blunted by a traditional American tactic. Early in the battle, some American sharp shooters succeeded in killing General Ross while he directed his men from the back of his horse. His successor was faced with stiff defenses and eventually withdrew.

Meanwhile, the navy tried to subdue Fort McHenry, which protected Baltimore harbor. The British bombarded the fort all during the night of September 13th to 14th. On board one of the British ships was a young American named Francis Scott Key. He had come aboard to negotiate for the release of a friend who had been captured a month before at the Battle of Bladensburg. He was detained during the attack on the fort. He watched most of the night in a state of high anxiety as the British pounded the fort with cannon fire. He was overjoyed when the first light of morning showed the Stars and Stripes still flying over the fort. He wrote out a poem in honor of the event which was set to the music of an English drinking song. It eventually became our national anthem, "The Star-Spangled Banner."

Key's poem celebrated the failure of the British assault on Baltimore. The army reboarded the ships after they had given up on the well-fortified Fort McHenry. The entire force withdrew from the region about a month later.

Treaty of Ghent. The British, who were expecting news of victories, were upset by reports of the failures in New York and Baltimore. The government offered the Duke of Wellington, the great British commander who had defeated Napoleon, a chance to take over the campaign in America. He informed the government that the only way to defeat the United States would be to control the Great Lakes. That would mean building a large fleet that could never be used on the ocean. As badly as the British wanted to teach the Americans a lesson, the cost was too high. Britain was exhausted and in deep financial trouble after twenty years of war in Europe. Napoleon was still alive and might return. (He did in 1815). The negotiators at Ghent were ordered to make a reasonable peace.

The two sides agreed to a return to the **status quo**. The fighting ended, and both sides retained the land they had when the war began. The Americans did not demand any statement or concession on the issues of impressment or ship seizures; the completion of the war in Europe had ended them anyway. In turn the British gave up their captured territory. They were never again to be an issue in British-American relations.

News of the Treaty of Ghent, signed in December of 1814, took several weeks to reach the United States. In those few weeks, the biggest land battle of the war was fought. The long-anticipated British invasion from the West Indies had finally taken place at New Orleans. The new peace started off quite unexpectedly.

Oh, say can you see by the dawn's early light
What so proudly we hailed at the twilight's last gleaming?
Whose broad stripes and bright stars thro' the perilous fight,
O'er the ramparts we watched were so gallantly streaming?
And the rocket's red glare, the bombs bursting in air,
Gave proof thro' the night that our flag was still there.
Oh, say does that star-spangled banner yet wave
O'er the land of the free and the home of the brave?

On the shore, dimly seen through the mists of the deep,
Where the foe's haughty host in dread silence reposes,
What is that which the breeze, o'er the towering steep,
As it fitfully blows, half conceals, half discloses?
Now it catches the gleam of the morning's first beam,
In full glory reflected now shines in the stream:
Tis the star-spangled banner! Oh long may it wave
O'er the land of the free and the home of the brave.

And where is that band who so vauntingly swore
That the havoc of war and the battle's confusion,
A home and a country should leave us no more!
Their blood has washed out their foul footsteps' pollution.
No refuge could save the hireling and slave,
From the terror of flight and the gloom of the grave:
And the star-spangled banner in triumph doth wave
O'er the land of the free and the home of the brave.

Oh! thus be it ever, when freemen shall stand
Between their loved home and the war's desolation!
Blest with victory and peace, may the Heav'n-rescued land
Praise the Pow'r that hath made and preserved us a nation.
Then conquer we must, when our cause it is just,
And this be our motto: "In God is our trust."
And the star-spangled banner in triumph shall wave
O'er the land of the free and the home of the brave.

THE STAR-SPANGLED BANNER
by Francis Scott Key

Answer these questions.

3.19 Why did the military situation change in 1814?

_____

3.20 What did the British negotiators demand when the two sides first met at Ghent in August of

1814? _____

_____

_____

3.21 Why did the demands of the British change by December of 1814?

_____

3.22 What was the British strategy in the War of 1812?

_____

3.23 Who faced the British at the Battle of Bladensburg?

_____

3.24 Who led the American negotiators at Ghent? _____

3.25 What eastern state did Britain occupy part of during the war? _____

3.26 How did the British end their embarrassing string of naval losses?

_____

3.27 What naval battle turned back the British advance into New York, and who was the American
commander?

_____

3.28 What did the British do in Washington in August of 1814?

_____

3.29 How did the British attack Baltimore?

_____

3.30 The "Star-Spangled Banner" was written about the defense of what?

_____

3.31 What two battles were fought during America's last invasion of Canada?

_____

3.32 What was the basic result of the Treaty of Ghent?

_____

Rewrite the first and last verse of the "Star-Spangled Banner" in prose, plainly writing what the author was saying.

3.33 _____

_____

_____

_____

_____

_____

_____

_____

_____

_____

_____

_____

_____

_____

_____

_____

_____

_____

_____

_____

_____

Write a two-page biography of any of these people, using at least three sources.

George Washington	John Adams	Thomas Jefferson
James Madison	Alexander Hamilton	Henry Knox
James Monroe	Aaron Burr	Abigail Adams
Dolley Madison	Martha Washington	John Jay
John Marshall	Meriwether Lewis	William Clark

TEACHER CHECK _____ _____
                    initials   date

Results

Andrew Jackson. The Creek People of the southeast Mississippi took advantage of the war in 1813 to attack and massacre the defenders of Fort Mims near Mobile, Alabama. The Creek People were certain to assist the British when they attacked in the south. Andrew Jackson, a senator from Tennessee and commander of the state militia, moved south to confront the Creek People. He led a well-organized, ruthless, and decisive campaign. After Jackson's victory at the Battle of Horseshoe Bend in March of 1814, he forced the Creek to concede a huge portion of territory that included much of the states of Georgia and Alabama. Impressed with Jackson's results, the secretary of war gave him command of the American army in the south in 1814.

The Americans knew the British were preparing a large army in the West Indies to gain control of the lower Mississippi. Jackson moved into Spanish Florida and took the city of Pensacola in November, cutting off an excellent invasion route for the British. Then he began to prepare for an invasion along the Gulf Coast. When the British landed near New Orleans, Jackson came in to defend the city.

Battle of New Orleans. Jackson set up a strong defensive position in front of the advancing British in the swampy land around the mouth of the Mississippi. His men built fortifications of logs and dirt on a platform of cotton bales and wood. The position was located with a swamp on one side and the Mississippi River on the other. The enemy could not easily go around them. The barricade was manned by about 7,000 men, including soldiers, free blacks, backwoodsmen, pirates, and Frenchmen.

The over-confident British with an army of 10,000, including many veterans of the Napoleonic Wars, decided on a frontal attack. On the morning of January 8, 1815 (two weeks after the Treaty of Ghent had been signed), the British marched straight at the Americans in formation. The Americans mowed them down like grass. Over 2,000 British soldiers were killed or wounded while the Americans lost less than fifty. It was the greatest American victory of the war, even if it did come after the war ended. It also made Andrew Jackson a national hero.

News of the victory reached the cities of the east coast just before news of the treaty in Europe. Americans went wild with joy. They had not lost any territory in the treaty, and they had a great victory to cap it off. The public rejoiced using the slogan, "Not One Inch of Territory Ceded or Lost." The American perception of the war was that they had won.

The Hartford Convention. New England, under Federalist leadership, continued to oppose the war right up to the end. Five of the New England states sent representatives, who were Federalists, to a meeting in Hartford, Connecticut in December of 1814 to discuss their grievances and options. Their continued opposition to the war led many people to question their loyalty. The secret meetings in December and January caused further concern.

The Hartford Convention issued a report requesting several changes in the basic structure of the government. The changes would have increased the power of the states at the

| The British, in formation, marching towards the Americans

expense of the federal government. The recommendations included restrictions on the federal government's ability to make war or restrict trade, both key New England issues. The Convention wanted the states to have more control over their own defense. They also wanted to increase New England's power in the national government by making the admission of new states more difficult.

The report of the Convention was taken to Washington by three special envoys from Massachusetts. They arrived in the capital about the same time as the news of the Battle of New Orleans and the Treaty of Ghent. Their proposals were ridiculed and they left in disgrace. The popular reaction against the Federalist proposals cost them what was left of their strength. They only nominated one more presidential candidate in 1816 before they disappeared into historical extinction.

Results of the War. The end of the war marked a turning point in British-American relations. Four boundary disputes between the two nations were referred to **arbitration** for solutions. All disputes in the future between America and the former mother country would be settled by negotiations, not war. Over the next years and decades, steps were taken to remove border forts and warships on the Great Lakes between the U.S. and Canada. Eventually, the two neighbors would come to share the longest unfortified boundary in the world. Feelings still ran high against the British for many years, but the journey down the long path to friendship had begun.

The major Native American threat of the frontier was extinguished during the War of 1812. Tecumseh's confederacy was destroyed at the Battle of the Thames, and the Native American Peoples of the south were subdued in the Battle of Horseshoe Bend. Both groups were forced to cede large areas of land to the U.S. government. The pioneers quickly began to migrate to the new areas, creating more states for the Union. Indiana, Mississippi, Alabama,

and Illinois were added to the nation within five years after the war.

The great manufacturing power of the United States was born as a result of the War of 1812. The war and trade embargoes had drastically cut imports from Europe and deprived wealthy Americans of their major investment, which was commerce. Many wealthy men, especially in New England, invested their idle money in building factories of their own to produce goods the nation could not get from Europe. Out of necessity, the engine of American manufacturing began.

The Second War for Independence gave the nations of Europe a new respect for the young nation. British naval officers no longer sneered at American ships and seamen. European powers no longer tried to get some of the new nation's land for themselves. The war had ended their hopes that the nation would fall apart, leaving them to pick up the richest pieces.

The War of 1812 marked the end of the nation's dangerous infancy. The first leaders had kept the peace long enough for the nation to gain the strength needed to fight alone. Americans had held their own against the greatest power of Europe and proved their mettle in battle. The war gave them a new sense of their own destiny which they believed was to expand their republic across the width of the continent.

Florida. After the war, Florida was the only land east of the Mississippi not in American hands. The proud Yankees wanted it and believed it was destined by Providence to be theirs. Andrew Jackson had already seized parts of West Florida during the War of 1812. Afterwards, the Americans **annexed** that land and opened negotiations with Spain for the rest of it.

Spain was reluctant to sell Florida. She had her own agenda and resented America's presence in West Florida. The Spanish government wanted to settle the boundaries of the whole Louisiana Territory and did not want America to support the rebelling Spanish colonies in Latin

America. Circumstances, in the form of Andrew Jackson, forced Spain to negotiate.

In the years after the war, Native Americans, runaway slaves, and thieves began using Florida as a base for raids into the United States. In 1818 the president sent Andrew Jackson "to deal with the Seminole People," who were using Florida as a base. Jackson interpreted his orders liberally and marched into Florida where he defeated the Seminoles. He also captured St. Marks and Pensacola, executing two British citizens who were aiding the Native American People.

The raids by Jackson convinced the Spanish government that they could not successfully defend Florida. Therefore, in 1819 they signed the Adams-Onis Treaty that ceded it to the United States. The treaty also settled the boundaries of the Louisiana Territory with Spain giving up all of its claim to the Oregon country. The United States agreed that Texas was Spanish territory and took responsibility for about 5 million dollars in claims that U.S. citizens had against Spain. The northern and southern bounds of the U.S. were now set. The only direction left to go was west.

Complete these sentences.

3.34 The Battle of New Orleans made _____ a national hero.

3.35 The Federalists destroyed the last of their party with the proposals that were made at the _____ at the end of the War of 1812.

3.36 Andrew Jackson was given command of the army in 1814 after his success as a military commander against the _____ People.

3.37 The Battle of New Orleans took place _____ after the Treaty of Ghent was signed.

3.38 Jackson captured part of western _____ during the war and the American government later annexed it.

3.39 The Creek People were defeated at the Battle of _____ .

3.40 The Spanish government agreed to cede Florida after _____ made raids into the territory against the _____ People.

3.41 America obtained Florida and settled the boundaries of the Louisiana Territory by the _____ Treaty of 1819.

3.42 The lack of trade encouraged many wealthy New Englanders to invest in _____ during the War of 1812.

3.43 The Treaty of Ghent settled four boundary disputes by referring them to _____ .

3.44 The War of 1812 gave the nations of Europe a new _____ for the United States.

Answer these questions.

3.45 How did British-American relations change after the War of 1812?

_____

_____

_____

3.46 Why could pioneers flood onto the frontier after the war?

_____

_____

3.47 What mistake did the British make at New Orleans?

_____

_____

3.48 Who did the American public believe won the War of 1812?

_____

_____

3.49 What did America believe was its destiny?

_____

_____

Good Feelings

Nationalism. The War of 1812 produced a new feeling of **nationalism** in America. The nation believed that it had won a war against Great Britain. After that, the proud American navy thrashed the Barbary pirates so completely that all tribute payments were ended. The regional outlook of the New England Federalists had been discredited. Citizens of the United States began to think of themselves as just that—U.S. citizens. The older view that they were citizens of a state that was part of a Union declined for a time. This also led to a respect for the ideal of the "common man," the founder and defender of the great American republic.

The American System. Speaker of the House Henry Clay captured the pulse of the nation with his "American System." The American System was a group of proposals intended to benefit the entire nation. It included a protective tariff, a new national bank, money for roads and canals, and other improvements. Some of it became law.

The tariff was included in the American System in order to protect infant American factories that were born during the war. British manufacturers had not been able to sell their goods during the war, so they had collected their huge surpluses in warehouses, waiting to be sold. Once the Treaty of Ghent was signed, England began shipping boatloads of goods to America. Prices were driven so low that American factories were going out of business. In 1816 Congress passed the first protective tariff. It was different from earlier ones which were small and used to raise money. These new tariffs were high—20 to 25%—and were intended to make foreign goods more expensive so American goods could compete.

The absence of a national bank proved to be a disaster for the nation's finances. Any bank could print money, and many did, printing more than they could redeem in gold or silver. This made the currency decline rapidly in value,

causing inflation. Financial chaos had been a particular problem during the war. Under the leadership of Clay and Calhoun, a Second National Bank was chartered in 1816. The Democratic-Republicans had learned their lesson and supported it.

The Second National Bank was even larger than the first. Unfortunately, it got off to a bad start. The managers of the bank printed money freely, made loans improperly, and **speculated** in western land (a popular occupation at the time). The bank's new president, Nicholas Biddle, took over in 1819 and brought the institution under control. He reset policies, recalled risky loans, and reduced the money printed to match the gold reserves. The sudden change in policy was good for the bank, but it hurt the nation as a whole. It contributed to the Panic of 1819 (panic was a name for a **depression**). The bank foreclosed on many farms, especially in the west, which hurt its popular support.

The last part of Clay's American System was the proposal to use the extra revenue from the higher tariffs to build roads and canals. Clay believed that desperately needed improvements in transportation would allow western and southern farmers to increase their trade with the manufacturers of the north, benefiting everyone. One such road had already begun. The first national road, the Cumberland Road, was begun in 1811. It ran from Cumberland, Maryland to Vandalia, Illinois. It eventually connected to St. Louis on the Mississippi.

However, most of the improvements were needed inside the states, not between them. President Madison, and later Monroe, believed it was unconstitutional to use federal funds to benefit projects in one state, even if it would benefit the nation as a whole. So when Congress passed the Bonus Bill in 1817 (which would have given money from the new National Bank to the states for improvements), Madison vetoed it. The states were forced to finance the roads and canals themselves. Many did so by encouraging private citizens to build roads and charge for their use. These "turnpikes" spread all over the nation.

Era of Good Feelings. In 1816 James Monroe was elected president. He crushed his Federalist opponent 183 to 34 in the electoral vote. Monroe was the last president to have served in the Revolution and the last of the "Virginia Dynasty" (Washington, Jefferson, Madison, Monroe). He joined the army at eighteen and fought in several major battles of the Revolution, including Trenton where he was wounded in the shoulder. His political career included the Virginia legislature, the Confederation Congress, governor of Virginia, envoy to France and Britain, U.S. senator, as well as secretary of state and secretary of war under Madison. His appearance and manners resembled those of George Washington. He established a strict protocol for social events, following Washington's example. He was not a brilliant leader, but was a capable, experienced administrator who knew how to listen for "the will of the people."

James Monroe took over a nation still basking in the glow of the War of 1812. There was only one major political party, the

Democratic-Republicans, and the nation was united as never before. Shortly after his election, Monroe took a tour of the country. He was greeted with widespread acclaim, even in New England. One newspaper spoke of an "Era of Good Feelings" that had come over America. This era lasted through much of the early part of the Monroe administration but gradually yielded to the rise of sectionalism which will be covered in the next LIFEPAC. However, the "good feelings" lasted until Monroe's re-election in 1820. He ran unopposed and won every electoral vote except one. That one was deliberately thrown away so that the honor of being unanimously elected would fall only on George Washington.

Western Land. The United States of America is a land whose national character and history were built on the frontier. From the time the first settlers arrived in 1603 until the early 1900s, the nation always was expanding into the frontier. The frontier changed from the east coast, to the foothills of the Appalachians, to the eastern Mississippi, to the west coast, and lastly, to the Great Plains. For much of our history the acquisition of new lands, the settling of that land, and the addition of new states have been major political issues in Washington.

| A log cabin on the frontier

The frontier of the Era of Good Feelings was the eastern Mississippi. This frontier saw huge gains in population after the war. The population of the territory/state of Illinois in 1820 was more than four times what it had been in 1810. In that same time period, the population of Kentucky and Mississippi more than doubled while that of Illinois multiplied four times and Alabama increased thirteen times over!

The move west was encouraged by increasingly easy terms to purchase government land. The Land Ordinance of 1795 had set the price at $1 per acre payable in two installments with a minimum purchase of 640 acres. In 1800 the law was changed to a minimum purchase of 320 acres and four payments. By 1804 the price was $2 an acre, but the minimum purchase was only 160 acres. After the Panic of 1819, further reductions were made in 1820. The price was reduced to $1.25 an acre with an 80-acre minimum, and the purchaser could keep whatever part of the land he managed to pay for, only losing the unpaid portion. These generous terms kept the American population moving west to claim land of their own.

The Marshall Court. John Marshall remained chief justice of the Supreme Court for thirty-four years (1801-1835). He used his position to pursue the Hamilton-Federalist goals of a strong central government and protection against the excesses of democracy. Using its self-created right to judicial review, the Marshall Court issued a series of important decisions.

Fletcher v. Peck (1810) was a suit brought after the Georgia legislature sold 35 million acres of land to speculators in a corrupt deal. In its next session, the legislature revoked the deal due to public outcry. Marshall ruled that it was a contract and could not be arbitrarily revoked. He placed property rights, even dubious ones, above the power of the legislature. He asserted the Supreme Court's right to declare *state* laws unconstitutional.

McCulloch v. Maryland (1819) was a suit over the right of the states to tax the National Bank. Following the Panic of 1819, popular opinion ran high against the bank. Maryland tried to destroy it by taxing it out of existence. Marshall ruled that the federal government had the right to create the bank under its implied powers in the Constitution (loose construction), and the states had no authority to tax the federally created National Bank.

Many other decisions followed the same lines of reasoning. States were not allowed to change the charter of a college after *Dartmouth College v. Woodard* (1819), because it was a contract and was protected by the Constitution. The decision in *Cohens v. Virginia* (1821) gave the Supreme Court the right to reverse the decisions of even the highest state courts. The court ruled in *Gibbons v. Ogden* (1824) that only the federal government could regulate interstate commerce. Elected officials who favored state's rights and the power of the legislature objected to these rulings but could not find any way to effectively challenge them.

Monroe Doctrine. The aftermath of the Napoleonic Wars restored the old monarchs of Europe to their thrones. From then on, these rulers were determined to stop any and all revolutions like the one in France. Rebellions in favor of democracy were crushed by an alliance of monarchs in both Italy and Spain in the early 1820s. The United States began to fear that the new republics in Latin America that had recently won their freedom from Spain might suffer a similar fate. Americans naturally favored the new republics as followers of their own example. The presence of large European armies in the Americas would have been a definite threat to the United States.

The U.S. had an unexpected ally in their support for the new republics. Britain was enjoying the new freedom she had in trading with Latin America. This had previously been restricted by

Spain. Britain proposed that she and the U.S. issue a joint statement against any European intervention. However, Secretary of State John Quincy Adams was suspicious of the motives behind Britain's offer. He saw no reason for the U.S. to ride behind British foreign policy.

At the urging of Adams, Monroe decided to follow a separate but parallel course with the British. He took advantage of his annual address to Congress in 1823 to announce the American policy which became known as the Monroe Doctrine. He stated, the American continents were closed to any further European colonization. An attempt by the powers of the Old World to intervene in America would be viewed as a hostile act against the United States. Furthermore, the U.S. would not interfere with any European colonies already in America, nor would she intervene in European conflicts.

The United States lacked the military strength to back up this sweeping statement. It was largely ignored outside the country, but American national pride supported the independent spirit in which it was made. In later years, when America had grown to be an international power, the Monroe Doctrine would become a major part of the nation's foreign policy.

Conclusion. The years from 1789 to the early 1820s were a time of foundation building in the United States. The institutions of the new republic were established along with the customs and protocols that accompany them. The nation faced and successfully completed a peaceful change of political authority in 1800. The power of government was reaching down towards the people and away from the elites. The nation's leaders remained calm in the light of severe provocation from Europe as the Napoleonic Wars raged. Finally, when they could stand no more, America had fought again for her independence, this time from the arrogance of the British. The nation came out of the war with her territory and pride intact. The east coast from Canada to Mexico was under her control, and the west called to her growing population. Finally, America boldly asserted her right to keep the Old World out of her neighborhood. The foundation was laid. Its strength would be tested by fire in the decades ahead.

 Complete the following.

3.50 What were the three parts of Henry Clay's American System?

a. _____ b. _____

c. _____

3.51 What was the minimum number of acres of western land that had to be purchased in each year?

a. 1795 _____ b. 1800 _____

c. 1804 _____ d. 1820 _____

3.52 What was the time after the election of James Monroe called?

_____

3.53 Name the Supreme Court decision that decided each issue.

    a. College charters are contracts protected by the Constitution

    _____

    b. States can not tax a federal bank

    _____

    c. Only the federal government can regulate interstate trade

    _____

    d. Legislatures can not revoke a contract they made earlier, even if it was dubious

    _____

    e. The Supreme Court can reverse the decision of the highest state courts

    _____

3.54 Name the four parts of the Monroe Doctrine.

    a. _____

    b. _____

    c. _____

    d. _____

3.55 What was the sentiment of the nation after the War of 1812? _____

3.56 What part of the American System was opposed by Presidents Madison and Monroe? Why?

_____

_____

3.57 Who brought the Second National Bank under better management?
What was the name of the depression caused by his tightened monetary policies?

    a. _____   b. _____

3.58 What was the American frontier of the early 1800s? _____

3.59 What major European nation supported the new Latin American republics?

_____

3.60 Who was the chief justice of the Supreme Court from 1801 to 1835?
Whose ideas of government did he promote?

    a. _____   b. _____

3.61 Why was the National Bank unpopular after 1819, especially in the west?

_____

_____

3.62 Name the first national road, the year it was begun, and the cities it eventually ran between.

a. _____ b. _____

c. _____

3.63 What were privately built roads which charged people to use them? _____

Before you take this last Self Test, you may want to do one or more of these self checks.

1. _____ Read the objectives. See if you can do them.
2. _____ Restudy the material related to any objectives that you cannot do.
3. _____ Use the **SQ3R** study procedure to review the material:
   a. **S**can the sections.
   b. **Q**uestion yourself.
   c. **R**ead to answer your questions.
   d. **R**ecite the answers to yourself.
   e. **R**eview areas you did not understand.
4. _____ Review all vocabulary, activities, and Self Tests, writing a correct answer for every wrong answer.

SELF TEST 3

Answer these questions (each answer, 4 points).

3.01 What was the main object of American strategy in the War of 1812?

_____

3.02 What are two of the things the British negotiators demanded when they first met with the Americans in Ghent in the summer of 1814?

a. _____ b. _____

3.03 What were the three parts of Henry Clay's proposed American System?

a. _____ b. _____

c. _____

3.04 What were two of the grievances that led to the War of 1812?

a. _____ b. _____

3.05 What were two of the parts of Alexander Hamilton's financial program?

a. _____ b. _____

Name the item described (each answer, 3 points).

3.06 _____ European interference in the Americas would be viewed as a hostile act by the U.S.

3.07 _____ Greatest American victory of the War of 1812, fought after the treaty was signed

3.08 _____ City burned by the British in the Chesapeake Bay campaign of 1814

3.09 _____ Political party that dominated the American government in the early 1800s

3.010 _____ Section of the country that opposed the War of 1812

3.011 _____ Group of Federalists who wanted to weaken the federal government near the end of the War of 1812

3.012 _____ Name given to the early part of the Monroe Administration because of the unity and good will of the nation

3.013 _____ A revolt against the excise tax in Pennsylvania under Washington

3.014 _____ "Old Ironsides," famous American frigate

3.015 _____ Song written about the siege of Fort McHenry in Baltimore

Match these people (each answer, 2 points).

3.016 _____ Andrew Jackson   a. American victor at the Battle of Lake Erie

3.017 _____ Henry Clay   b. American victor at the Battle of the Thames

3.018 _____ James Calhoun   c. Speaker of the House from Kentucky

3.019 _____ William H. Harrison   d. militia general, defeated the Creek People

3.020 _____ James Madison   e. chief justice of the Supreme Court

3.021 _____ Nicholas Biddle   f. British commander in Canada

3.022 _____ John Marshall   g. War Hawk from South Carolina

3.023 _____ William Hull   h. president of the Second National Bank

3.024 _____ Isaac Brock   i. president who asked for war with Britain

3.025 _____ Oliver Perry   j. American general, surrendered Detroit

Answer true or false (each answer, 1 point).

3.026 _____ The War of 1812 is also called the Second War for Independence.

3.027 _____ British navy was reduced in effectiveness by American naval victories in the War of 1812.

3.028 _____ American ships could not fight effectively against British ships.

3.029 _____ The British strategy in the War of 1812 was to capture key American cities and make the nation a colony again.

3.030 _____ The Battle of Plattsburgh Bay stopped the British invasion of New York coming down Lake Champlain.

3.031 _____ Americans were relieved and humiliated after the War of 1812.

3.032 _____ The War of 1812 encouraged the beginning of American manufacturing.

3.033 _____ America lost part of the Northwest Territory in the Treaty of Ghent.

3.034 _____ The military situation became worse for the Americans in 1814 when Napoleon went into exile.

3.035 _____ The steady improvement of British-American relations began after the War of 1812.

80 / 100	SCORE _____	TEACHER _____ _____
		initials date

Before taking the LIFEPAC Test, you may want to do one or more of these self checks.

1. _____ Read the objectives. See if you can do them.
2. _____ Restudy the material related to any objectives that you cannot do.
3. _____ Use the **SQ3R** study procedure to review the material.
4. _____ Review activities, Self Tests, and LIFEPAC vocabulary words.
5. _____ Restudy areas of weakness indicated by the last Self Test.